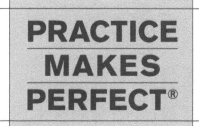

PRACTICE
MAKES
PERFECT®

Intermediate English Reading and Comprehension

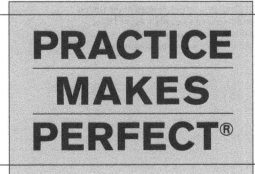

PRACTICE
MAKES
PERFECT®

Intermediate English Reading and Comprehension

Diane Engelhardt

Mc
Graw
Hill
Education

New York Chicago San Francisco Athens London Madrid
Mexico City Milan New Delhi Singapore Sydney Toronto

Copyright © 2013 by McGraw-Hill Education LLC. All rights reserved. Printed in the United States of America. Except as permitted under the United States Copyright Act of 1976, no part of this publication may be reproduced or distributed in any form or by any means, or stored in a database or retrieval system, without the prior written permission of the publisher.

2 3 4 5 6 7 QVS/QVS 20 19 18 17 16

ISBN   978-0-07-179884-6
MHID   0-07-179884-6

e-ISBN   978-0-07-179885-3
e-MHID   0-07-179885-4

Library of Congress Control Number 2012951207

McGraw-Hill Education, the McGraw-Hill Education logo, Practice Makes Perfect, and related trade dress are trademarks or registered trademarks of McGraw-Hill Education and/or its affiliates in the United States and other countries and may not be used without written permission. All other trademarks are the property of their respective owners. McGraw-Hill Education is not associated with any product or vendor mentioned in this book.

Interior design by Village Bookworks, Inc.

McGraw-Hill Education products are available at special quantity discounts to use as premiums and sales promotions or for use in corporate training programs. To contact a representative, please e-mail us at bulksales@mcgraw-hill.com.

This book is printed on acid-free paper.

Contents

Contents

Preface

Practice Makes Perfect: Intermediate English Reading and Comprehension contains 15 reading texts about unusual and amazing topics. The book is designed to:

◆ Build your English vocabulary
◆ Develop reading comprehension skills at an intermediate level
◆ Stimulate further investigation into the topics presented

This workbook is directed at the English language learner at the intermediate level—the student in a classroom looking for extra practice, as well as the independent learner practicing at his or her own pace.

Each chapter contains the following sections:

1. **Pre-reading** As an introduction to the topic, students who are learning in a classroom setting can answer questions or engage in a short discussion.
2. **Reading text** Following the theme of "find out about it," the stories—each between 1,000 and 1,600 words long—cover a broad range of topics of international appeal. They originate in the United States, Canada, Great Britain, Australia, Germany, Japan, and Australia.
3. **Vocabulary** Understanding and learning vocabulary can be difficult. You will find lots of new words in each text, and since not every new word can be included in a vocabulary list or exercise, you are encouraged to use an English-language dictionary and to keep an independent vocabulary journal to record new words. The exercises are broken down as follows.
    ◆ **Organizing vocabulary** An effective way to increase vocabulary is to learn words in association with other words—that is, to organize words according to subject matter. For example, in the reading about the Findhorn Community, there are many words that relate to gardening and spirituality.
    ◆ **Understanding vocabulary** Each chapter focuses on 15 words, which are in bold type in the reading text. You will master not only each word's synonyms and/or dictionary definition, but also its part of speech (noun, adjective, verb, idiom, phrase). Example: *competition* (n.), *competitive* (adj.), *compete* (v.).
    ◆ **Using vocabulary** A variety of exercises help you learn to use the 15 words in sentences.
4. **Reading comprehension** Comprehension exercises differ from chapter to chapter under the following headings:
    ◆ Reading for main ideas
    ◆ Reading for details
    ◆ Reading for facts and figures
    ◆ Reading for meaning

5. **Reading skills** In this section, you will learn to summarize the main ideas in the reading text. Exercises include outlines, timelines, profiles, charts, diaries, and short summaries in the form of newspaper articles and interviews.
6. **Web search and writing** In this two-page exercise, you can work with a study partner and further develop your reading skills by searching the Web for information about the topic. A short writing exercise concludes the web search.

An answer key is provided at the end of the book with answers to the exercises in the Vocabulary and Reading comprehension sections.

◆ ◆ ◆

Reading is a great source of knowledge, but—more than providing facts, figures, and a wealth of information—reading can take us on journeys to places we might never see and introduce us to people we could never meet in person. The amazing stories in this book were written not only for your skill development but also for your pleasure. Read them and enjoy!

Acknowledgments

I thank: Tom Ryan of the Royal Flying Doctors Service; Carin Bolles and Judy McAllister of the Findhorn Community for their helpful feedback; my editor, Holly McGuire, for her guidance; and my husband, Erich, for his support.

PRACTICE
MAKES
PERFECT®

Intermediate English Reading and Comprehension

Bananas about bananas ◆·1·

Pre-reading

Which fruit is the healthiest? Rate each of these fruits from 1 to 10, according to how healthy you think each is.

_____ Apples   _____ Oranges

_____ Bananas   _____ Peaches

_____ Grapes   _____ Pears

_____ Kiwi   _____ Pineapple

_____ Mangoes   _____ Plums

_____ Melons   _____ Strawberries

Reading text

1   An apple a day keeps the doctor away. In winter, the antioxidant vitamin C in oranges and citrus fruits **boosts** the immune system. Grapes are high in **nutrients**; vitamins B_1, B_2, B_6, C, and K; and essential minerals. Pineapple is a natural healer **packed with** vitamin C and bromelain, a potential anti-inflammatory. The list of healthy, healing fruits goes on and on, but when it comes to health, popularity, **versatility**, and overall usefulness, none can beat the banana.

History and cultivation

2   Bananas **originated in** Malaysia as early as 2000 BC, but the first banana plantations were established in China around 200 AD. In the early 1500s, the Portuguese and Spanish introduced bananas to the Caribbean and Americas. The United Fruit Company, formed in 1899, was responsible for the **commercialization** of Latin American bananas and controlled most of the trade in tropical fruit into the mid-twentieth century. Nowadays, bananas are traded as a **commodity**. With the aid of refrigerated transport, bananas have conquered the world.

3   According to the Food and Agriculture Organization of the United Nations, India is the world's top producer of bananas, with a total **output** of 21.7 metric tons in 2007. China is second, with 8 metric tons. However, of the 130 countries that grow bananas, Mexico, Costa Rica, Brazil, Colombia, Ecuador, and the Philippines are the major commercial producers.

4   Bananas do not grow on a tree, as most people imagine, but on a sturdy plant that can reach 6 to 7.6 meters high, with large leaves up to 0.6 meters wide and 2.75 meters long. In fact, the banana plant, *Musa acuminata*, is the world's largest

perennial herb. Cultivation is best suited to tropical and subtropical areas with ample water, rich soil, and good drainage. Because bananas have been **cultivated** to become seedless, commercially grown bananas are **propagated** through division, a process of separating offshoots, or "pups," from the mother plant.

5   Classified as a berry rather than a fruit, the banana develops in a heart-shaped flower bud and forms **bunches**, called a "hand," of 10 to 20 individual "fingers" weighing 20 to 45 kilograms. Although we picture bananas in a bright yellow skin with brown spots, turning to a solid brownish black as they **ripen** and sweeten, they also come in green, purple, red, orange, pink, black, and striped jackets, and a variety of sizes. Of the 1,200 varieties of bananas, the most widely **consumed** banana is the Dwarf Cavendish (Cavendish for short), named for William Cavendish, 6th Duke of Devonshire, who cultivated an early specimen in his hothouses.

Nutritional composition

6   A nine-inch-long banana is 75 percent water and 35 percent skin, and has between 110 and 140 calories. Bananas contain three sugars: sucrose, fructose, and glucose, making them an instant and **sustained** energy food. The following table lists only some of the most important nutrients in a banana.

Nutrient	Amount
Carbohydrates	36 grams
Fiber	3–4 grams
Protein	2 grams
Fat	0.4 grams
Cholesterol	0
Vitamin C	13.8 mg
Calcium	9.2 mg
Magnesium	44.1 mg
Manganese	0.3 mg
Potassium	602 mg
Sodium	1–2 mg

(For a more exact, detailed breakdown, go to http://bananasweb.com/bananas-nutrition-facts.)

Health benefits

Heart protection and hemoglobin production

7   Because of their extremely high potassium and minimal sodium content, bananas have been proven to reduce the risk of high blood pressure and stroke, and to regulate heartbeat. The iron in bananas **ensures** the production of hemoglobin in the blood and prevents anemia.

Mental health and brain function

8   When converted into serotonin, the tryptophan in bananas can lift our spirits. The potassium in bananas helps relieve stress and heightens the ability to learn. The next time exams roll around, why not pack a banana with your books at study time?

Bone building

9   Fatty acids in green and ripe bananas, combined with fructooligosaccharides, allow our bodies to better absorb calcium, which is needed to build strong, healthy bones and prevent such debilitating conditions as osteoporosis in our later years. The manganese in bananas helps lubricate cartilage in the joints.

Kidney protection

10   Bananas contain antioxidant phenolic compounds, which detoxify the kidneys. The *International Journal of Cancer* has published research showing that women who eat bananas four to six times a week in addition to cabbage and root vegetables have a 40 percent lower risk of developing kidney cancer.

Digestion

11   Bananas help our bodies digest food by reducing acidity and irritation in the lining of the stomach; these can lead to the formation of painful ulcers. Bananas also keep digested food moving through the bowels, work as an antacid to relieve heartburn, and restore electrolytes, particularly potassium, after a bout of diarrhea.

Other benefits

12   Bananas can relieve or cure some less serious health problems, such as morning sickness, mosquito bites, and hangovers. Bananas can improve eyesight and help a person quit smoking. In dieting, a banana is a better choice to combat a craving for something sweet than chocolate or ice cream. About the only claim a banana can't make is to grow hair on a bald head (but maybe no one has tested that yet).

13   Although the banana peel is not eaten, its antifungal and antibiotic properties can soothe insect bites, relieve rashes and skin irritation, heal wounds, and help remove warts. The leaves also have medicinal qualities, but are more widely used in cooking food—and in providing shelter from rain and sun.

Final words

14   It's no wonder that people are "bananas" about bananas.[1] For all its many uses and amazing talents, the best thing to do with a banana is to eat it: with yogurt, ice cream, peanut butter, chocolate sauce, nuts and whipped cream, or just by itself. You can enjoy bananas all the more by knowing that you're doing something for your health!

---

[1] The slang expressions *to be bananas* and *to go bananas* mean to show extreme excitement, enthusiasm, or craziness about something.

Vocabulary

Organizing vocabulary *In the chart below, insert words and phrases from the following list under the appropriate headings. Include the part of speech (n. for noun, v. for verb) for each entry. An example has been provided for each heading.*

anemia	cure	prevent
antacid	detoxify	rash
anti-inflammatory	diarrhea	relieve
antibiotic properties	fatty acids	restore
antifungal properties	heal	serotonin
antioxidant	heart	soothe
bone	heartburn	stomach
bowels	high blood pressure	stress
brain	immune system	stroke
calcium	irritation	ulcer
cancer	kidney	wound
cartilage	osteoporosis	

Diseases and ailments	Parts of the body	Substances with a healthful effect	Medical treatments
high blood pressure (n.)	*heart (n.)*	*antioxidant (n.)*	*prevent (v.)*
_____	_____	_____	_____
_____	_____	_____	_____
_____	_____	_____	_____
_____	_____	_____	_____
_____	_____	_____	_____
_____	_____	_____	_____
_____	_____		
_____			
_____			
_____			

EXERCISE
1·2

Understanding and using vocabulary *For each word or phrase in the following list, indicate its part of speech (n. for noun, v. for verb, adj. for adjective). Then, for each numbered item that follows, choose the appropriate word or phrase from the list as a replacement for the underlined word or phrase. Be sure to use the correct form of each verb and to pluralize nouns, if necessary.*

boost _____   cultivate _____   packed with _____

bunch _____   ensure _____   propagate _____

commercialization _____   nutrients _____   ripen _____

commodity _____   originate in _____   sustain _____

consume _____   output _____   versatility _____

1. Fruit and vegetables are <u>full of</u> vitamins and antioxidants.

   _____

2. In North America, people <u>eat</u> tons of bananas every year.

   _____

3. The company's new advertising campaign <u>gave</u> its lagging sales <u>a big push</u>.

   _____

4. For many decades, farmers in the prairies have <u>raised</u> cereal crops, such as wheat, barley, and oats.

   _____

5. Tomatoes need a lot of sunlight to <u>develop and be ready to be eaten</u>.

   _____

6. The banana <u>first came from</u> Malaysia.

   _____

7. That <u>set</u> of grapes <u>growing together</u> looks delicious.

   _____

8. It is important to eat food that contains lots of <u>substances that provide nourishment</u>.

   _____

9. In order to stay healthy, you have to <u>make certain</u> that you eat fresh produce and grains, and limit your intake of animal fats.

   _____

10. Most plants are <u>reproduced</u> from seed.

    _____

11. No one can <u>keep</u> himself <u>going</u> on water alone.

    _____

12. <u>Articles of trade</u>, such as coffee, sugar, and grain, are bought and sold daily on world markets.

_____

13. The <u>profitable marketing</u> of kiwi fruit has made it very popular outside New Zealand.

_____

14. Apples are known for their <u>many different uses</u> in baking.

_____

15. The annual <u>amount produced</u> of hydroelectric power will increase in the future.

_____

Reading comprehension

EXERCISE
1·3

Reading for main ideas *Indicate which of the following statements are true (T) and which are false (F).*

1. _____ Bananas are the most widely known and popular fruit.

2. _____ Bananas are cultivated in only a few tropical countries.

3. _____ Bananas come in many different colors and sizes.

4. _____ Bananas have a wide range of positive health benefits.

5. _____ Bananas have fewer health benefits than apples, grapes, and pineapple.

6. _____ Bananas are a great energy food.

7. _____ Bananas are good for the heart.

8. _____ There is no scientific evidence that bananas are good for our health.

9. _____ Bananas aid in digestion and waste elimination.

10. _____ The banana plant itself has no health benefits.

Reading for details *Choose the answer that correctly completes each of the following sentences.*

1. Bananas were first grown in _____.
   a. China
   b. Malaysia
   c. Spain and Portugal

2. Bananas were commercialized by _____.
   a. Portuguese and Spanish explorers
   b. Chinese fruit growers
   c. an American company

3. The most popular variety of banana is the _____.
   a. Cavendish
   b. Devonshire
   c. Costa Rican

4. Bananas are a good source of energy because they contain _____.
   a. lots of potassium
   b. three sugars
   c. Vitamin C

5. Bananas protect the heart because they are rich in _____.
   a. potassium
   b. sodium
   c. manganese

6. Bananas are good brain food because they can _____.
   a. lower blood pressure
   b. reduce stress
   c. help digest food better

7. Bananas help build bones because they allow bones to better absorb _____.
   a. calcium
   b. potassium
   c. manganese

8. Women who eat a lot of bananas have a lower risk of _____.
   a. breast cancer
   b. stomach cancer
   c. kidney cancer

9. The banana peel can be used to cure _____.
   a. skin irritations
   b. baldness
   c. cancer

10. It's okay to eat a banana when you are on a diet, because _____.
    a. it's easily digested
    b. it has only a few calories
    c. it contains antioxidants

Reading for facts and figures *Complete the chart below with facts and figures from the reading text.*

1. Average length of one banana _____

2. Water content (in percent) _____

3. Number of fingers in a hand _____

4. Weight of a hand _____

5. Average number of calories _____

6. Method of propagation _____

7. Maximum leaf size (width and length) _____

8. Height of a plant _____

9. Requirements for cultivation _____

10. Main banana-producing countries _____

11. Number of banana varieties _____

Reading for meaning *Would a health professional agree or disagree with the following statements? Indicate the number of the paragraph that supports your opinion.*

1. You should include bananas in your diet. Paragraph _____
   ☐ Agree
   ☐ Disagree
   ☐ Neither

2. If you are on a diet, you should avoid bananas. Paragraph _____
   ☐ Agree
   ☐ Disagree
   ☐ Neither

3. It's a good idea to eat a banana when you are studying for a test. Paragraph _____
   ☐ Agree
   ☐ Disagree
   ☐ Neither

4. If you have the blues, eating a banana can make you feel better. Paragraph _____
   ☐ Agree
   ☐ Disagree
   ☐ Neither

5. You should eat at least one banana a day. Paragraph _____
   ☐ Agree
   ☐ Disagree
   ☐ Neither

Reading skills

Outline *Complete the outline below with relevant information from the reading text.*

The health benefits of bananas

Heart and blood production

1. _____

2. _____

3. _____

4. _____

Mental health and brain function

1. _____

2. _____

Bone building

1. _____

2. _____

Kidney protection

1. _____

2. _____

Digestion

1. _____

2. _____

3. _____

Skin

1. _____

2. _____

3. _____

4. _____

Other

1. _____

2. _____

3. _____

Web search and writing

The activities on the next two pages prompt you to share information with a study partner and to search the Web for recipes that call for bananas. In North America, banana bread (or loaf) is a popular way to use overripe bananas. Try this healthy and tasty snack!

Whole wheat banana bread

2	cups whole wheat flour	2	eggs, slightly beaten
1	teaspoon baking soda	1	cup mashed banana (or more)
½	teaspoon salt	⅓	cup hot water
½	cup melted butter	½	cup walnuts
1	cup brown sugar	½	cup chocolate chips

1. Preheat oven to 325°F (160°C).
2. Mix flour, baking soda, and salt in a medium-sized bowl.
3. In a large bowl, stir melted butter and sugar.
4. Add eggs and bananas; stir until blended.
5. Stir flour mixture into liquid mixture, alternating with hot water.
6. Stir in walnuts and chocolate chips.
7. Spoon into a greased 5″ × 9″ loaf pan, and bake for 70 minutes or until done. (If a toothpick inserted in the center comes out clean, the loaf is done.)

Cooking and baking with bananas

ACTIVITY
1·1

Exchange experiences *Ask your partner the following questions, and add a question of your own.*

1. What is your favorite way to eat bananas?

   ☐ Banana and peanut butter sandwich
   ☐ Banana bread
   ☐ Banana cream pie
   ☐ Banana smoothie
   ☐ Banana split
   ☐ Frozen bananas with chocolate coating
   ☐ Fruit salad

   ☐ _____

2. How often do you eat bananas? Why do/don't you like bananas?

   _____

3. Your question _____

Discussion *Share your answers with another partner or with the whole group.*

ACTIVITY 1·2

Search the Web *Find delicious-sounding recipes that call for bananas, and record the information below.*

Name of recipe _____

URL www._____

Ingredients _____

_____

_____

_____

Name of recipe _____

URL www._____

Ingredients _____

_____

_____

_____

Name of recipe _____

URL www._____

Ingredients _____

_____

_____

_____

ACTIVITY 1·3

Writing *Write out the best recipe that you found, including instructions on how to prepare it. When and how would you serve it?*

Schloss Neuschwanstein
A king and his castle

Pre-reading

What types of historical buildings interest you? Which of the following historical buildings and monuments have you visited?

- ☐ Angkor Wat
- ☐ Buckingham Palace
- ☐ The Eiffel Tower
- ☐ The Great Wall of China
- ☐ Macchu Picchu

- ☐ The Parthenon
- ☐ The Pyramids of Giza
- ☐ The Roman Coliseum
- ☐ The Statue of Liberty
- ☐ The Taj Mahal

Which place(s) would you like to visit? _____

_____

Reading text

1   Schloss[1] Neuschwanstein is one of Europe's most popular castles. Located on a hill overlooking the village of Hohenschwangau, near the town of Füssen in southern Germany, this nineteenth-century castle attracts 1.3 million international tourists every year. Recognized as the model for Sleeping Beauty's Castle at Disneyland in Anaheim, California, Schloss Neuschwanstein must be seen to be believed, but to fully appreciate its "fairy tale" **mystique**, one must learn about the king who planned and built it.

2   Ludwig Otto Friedrich Wilhelm was born to Maximilian II of Bavaria and Princess Marie of Prussia on August 25, 1845, in Schloss Nymphenburg in Munich, the capital of Bavaria. His brother, Otto, was born three years later. At the age of 18, Ludwig took the throne after his father died of a sudden illness, and he **reigned** as King Ludwig II of Bavaria from 1864 to 1886. On January 22, 1867, he became engaged to Duchess Sophie Charlotte in Bavaria, but after 10 months he broke off the engagement. Ludwig never married or produced an **heir**, which in those days was unthinkable for a monarch. With the exception of a platonic friendship with Empress Elizabeth of Austria, Ludwig's closest friendships were with men.

3   As a child, Ludwig told his governess that he wanted to remain an eternal **enigma** to himself and others, and in this regard he succeeded. Ludwig spent most of his childhood in the gothic castle of Hohenschwangau, surrounded by frescoes of German sagas. He was raised with a strict sense of duty and a keen awareness of his royal status. His true interests, however, lay in poetry and theater, and he

_____

[1] *Schloss* is the German word for "castle" or "palace."

tended to spend more time alone **indulging** his fantasies than training to become a future king. Ludwig grew into a tall, slim, and handsome Prince Charming, with a shock of dark wavy hair, full pouting lips, and wide dreamy eyes that often gaze upward in portraits as if at a distant dream world. In his later years, Ludwig filled out and wore a goatee, and his youthful wistfulness matured into a stern **aloofness.**

4   Ludwig's lack of political experience and his shy nature made him ill-suited to the throne of Bavaria. In 1866, two years after his **coronation**, Ludwig experienced a humiliating defeat when he was forced into an alliance with Prussia against Austria. Feeling himself a mere political underling to his uncle, the King of Prussia, Ludwig began to pay more attention to his personal interests than to his duties. He was an enthusiastic fan of the composer Richard Wagner; three months after becoming king, Ludwig invited Wagner to court. Despite the ups and downs of their lifelong relationship, Ludwig sponsored Wagner lavishly and saved him from financial ruin. He also established Munich as the music capital of Europe.

5   Ludwig believed in a **holy** kingdom created through the grace of God, and he identified with larger-than-life heroes of Middle Age sagas and legends. To turn his fantasies into reality, Ludwig built beautiful castles, which strangers were not allowed to enter. In 1874, construction began on the relatively small, neo-French rococo Schloss Linderhof. The baroque royal palace of Herrenchiemsee, begun in 1878 and modeled on the Château de Versailles, was built on a scenic island in Lake Chiemsee.

6   The most private and personal of his projects was his third, Schloss Neuschwanstein. **Commissioned** in 1867, Schloss Neuschwanstein was built between 1869 and 1886 as Ludwig's personal retreat in the mountains. Dedicated to the genius of Richard Wagner, the castle was designed in the neoromantic style. The interior was ornately decorated with themes from *Parsifal* and *Lohengrin,* two of Richard Wagner's operas. Ludwig spared no expense or luxury; hundreds of craftsmen employed the most up-to-date methods of construction and used the finest materials. The castle's many **amenities** included a central heating system, running cold and hot water, flush toilets, an electric intercom system, a telephone, and a dumbwaiter to transport food from the kitchen to the dining room. In 1884, Ludwig moved into his private upper-story suite, but the rest of the castle remained an ongoing construction site. Of the 200 planned rooms, only 15 were completed, and to this day Schloss Neuschwanstein and Ludwig's other castles remain unfinished symphonies.

7   When Ludwig's personal finances ran dry, he borrowed heavily from foreign banks. Despite his mounting debt and contrary to the advice of his financial ministers, Ludwig took on more **opulent** projects, such as a Byzantine palace in the Graswangtal and a Chinese summer palace in Tyrol. He withdrew from public life, shirked his duties, and engaged in increasingly **eccentric** behavior that earned him the nickname "Mad King Ludwig." In 1875, he began sleeping during the day and being active at night. He traveled in elaborate coaches and sleighs, and he dressed in historical costumes.

8   On June 10, 1886, a government commission declared Ludwig insane, and he was **deposed**. On June 12, he was taken into custody and transported to Castle Berg on Lake Starnberg. The next day, Ludwig and Dr. Bernhard von Gudden, the physician who certified Ludwig as mentally ill without a psychiatric examination, went for a walk. Their bodies were later found near the lake shore, with their heads and shoulders above the shallow water. Despite the fact that Ludwig was known to be a strong swimmer and no water was found in his lungs, his death was recorded as suicide by drowning. No investigation was ever made into the suspicious circumstances surrounding the two men's deaths. Ludwig II was **interred** on June 19 in the crypt at St. Michael's Church in Munich.

9   Ludwig II of Bavaria remains to this day an enigma and a source of romance and much speculation. The subject of biographies and movies, he has become an idealized and tragic figure, much like a character in a gothic romance novel. One can come to various conclusions about the

man, but there is no doubt about his **legacy**. Seven weeks after Ludwig's death, Schloss Neuschwanstein was opened to the public and since then, it has become a national treasure. Every day of summer, an estimated 6,000 visitors pay a 12-euro admission to tour Ludwig's private quarters. His dream castle has more than repaid any debt that he owed to the state, and Schloss Neuschwanstein has earned him international respect and admiration.

Vocabulary

EXERCISE
2·1

Organizing vocabulary *List the words and phrases from the reading text that relate to the following categories. An example has been provided for each category.*

1. Royalty (9) _take the throne,_ _____

_____

2. Mystery (4) _mystique,_ _____

3. Crazy (4) _eccentric,_ _____

4. Story (4) _saga,_ _____

5. The arts (6) _frescoes,_ _____

_____

6. Build (6) _construction,_ _____

_____

7. Architectural style (5) _gothic,_ _____

8. Fancy (5) _lavish,_ _____

Understanding vocabulary *Complete the following chart with the correct forms of the words from the reading text.*

Noun	Adjective	Verb
1. _____	_____	indulge
2. _____	_____	reign
3. aloofness	_____	X
4. _____	X	commission
5. coronation	X	_____
6. _____	X	depose
7. _____	eccentric	X
8. enigma	_____	X
9. heir	X	_____
10. _____	holy	X
11. _____	X	inter
12. _____	opulent	X
13. amenity	X	X
14. legacy	X	X
15. mystique	_____	X

Using vocabulary *For each of the following sentences, choose the appropriate word from the chart in Exercise 2-2 as a replacement for the underlined word or phrase. Be sure to use the correct form of each verb and to pluralize nouns, if necessary.*

1. Many <u>sacred</u> places are located in the city of Jerusalem.

   _____

2. There is a definite <u>air of mystery</u> surrounding the Egyptian pyramids and the tombs of the pharaohs.

   _____

3. The city has <u>contracted with</u> a well-known sculptor to create a statue in honor of the Queen.

   _____

4. The new hotel and conference center offers a wide range of <u>useful features</u> for business travelers.

   _____

5. Queen Victoria of England <u>ruled as monarch</u> for 63 years and seven months.

   _____

6. In the past, members of aristocratic families were <u>buried</u> in a large family tomb.

   _____

7. The old lady who lives with 20 cats in the pink and green house is very <u>strange and unconventional</u>.

   _____

8. On special occasions such as Christmas and Thanksgiving, people like to <u>gratify their desires</u> and eat lots of fattening goodies and treats.

   _____

9. In Europe, tourists can visit many <u>luxurious</u> castles and theaters.

   _____

10. During the October Revolution in Russia, Czar Nicholas was <u>removed from power</u> and executed.

    _____

11. In their will, parents name their children as <u>persons entitled to property</u> to their estate.

    _____

12. None of the other students liked the new girl at first, because of her <u>distant and unsympathetic behavior</u>, but as it turned out, she was only shy.

    _____

13. The <u>crowning ceremony</u> of kings and queens in Great Britain has always taken place in Westminster Abbey.

    _____

14. There are many <u>puzzles and paradoxes</u> associated with the story of the lost city of Atlantis.

    _____

15. When Mother Teresa died, she left a <u>gift handed down to future generations</u> of human kindness and concern for the poor and sick.

    _____

Reading comprehension

EXERCISE
2·4

Reading for main ideas *Match each of the following statements with the corresponding paragraph of the reading text.*

_____ Paragraph 1

_____ Paragraph 2

_____ Paragraph 3

_____ Paragraph 4

_____ Paragraph 5

_____ Paragraph 6

_____ Paragraph 7

_____ Paragraph 8

_____ Paragraph 9

a. Despite his strict upbringing, Ludwig grows into a dreamy-eyed Prince Charming.
b. Ludwig's debts mount and his lifestyle becomes increasingly eccentric.
c. Schloss Neuschwanstein becomes Ludwig's lasting legacy.
d. Ludwig builds Schloss Neuschwanstein as his personal retreat and homage to Richard Wagner.
e. Ludwig shows more interest in the arts than in his royal duties.
f. A fairy tale castle is created by a fairy tale king.
g. Ludwig is removed from the throne and dies tragically.
h. Ludwig builds his personal kingdom of castles.
i. Ludwig Otto Friedrich Wilhelm becomes Ludwig II of Bavaria.

EXERCISE
2·5

Reading for details *Answer each of the following questions with information from the reading text. Try not to copy directly from the text.*

1. What were Ludwig's main interests?

_____

2. Why did Ludwig build such costly and opulent castles?

_____

3. Why did he build *Neuschwanstein*?

_____

4. What were some of the castle's amenities?

_____

5. How did Ludwig finance the construction of his castles?

_____

6. Why was Ludwig given the nickname of "Mad King Ludwig"?

_____

7. What behavior of his earned him this nickname?

_____

8. How did Ludwig die?

_____

_____

EXERCISE
2·6

Reading for facts and figures *Choose the boldface word or phrase that correctly completes each of the following statements.*

1. Every year, **6,000** | **1.3 million** tourists visit Schloss Neuschwanstein.

2. Schloss Neuschwanstein was used as a model for **Cinderella's** | **Sleeping Beauty's** castle at Disneyland.

3. Schloss Neuschwanstein was dedicated to the genius of German composer **Richard Wagner** | **Ludwig van Beethoven**.

4. Only **15** | **200** rooms have been completed in Schloss Neuschwanstein.

5. Schloss Neuschwanstein is located in **southern** | **northern** Germany.

6. Admission to Schloss Neuschwanstein costs **12 euros** | **12 dollars**.

7. Schloss Neuschwanstein was built in the **gothic** | **neoromantic** style.

8. Ludwig became king when he was **18** | **28**.

9. Ludwig was born in **Hohenschwangau** | **Munich**.

10. The baroque **royal palace of Herrenchiemsee** | **Schloss Linderhof** was modeled after the Château de Versailles.

EXERCISE
2·7

Reading for meaning *Based on information from the reading text, draw your own conclusions about Ludwig II. First, choose the boldface word or phrase that correctly completes each of the following statements. Then, indicate which paragraph in the reading text contains the relevant information and provides evidence for your conclusion.*

1. Ludwig **had** | **didn't have** many female admirers as a young man.

   Paragraph _____

2. Ludwig **wanted** | **didn't want** to become king.

   Paragraph _____

3. Ludwig **was** | **wasn't** murdered.

   Paragraph _____

4. Ludwig **was** | **wasn't** crazy.

Paragraph _____

5. Ludwig **entertained** | **didn't entertain** large groups of people in his castles.

Paragraph _____

6. Ludwig **was** | **wasn't** good at managing money.

Paragraph _____

7. Ludwig **was** | **wasn't** popular with the Bavarian government.

Paragraph _____

8. Ludwig **loved** | **hated** public life.

Paragraph _____

9. Ludwig **was** | **wasn't** a great king and military leader.

Paragraph _____

10. Ludwig **is** | **isn't** a popular historical figure today.

Paragraph _____

Reading skills

EXERCISE 2·8

Summary *Construct a timeline of Ludwig II's life and his castles.*

Year	Event/milestone
1845	
1864	
1866	
1867	
1869	
1874	
1875	
1878	
1884	
1886	

Web search and writing

The activities on the next two pages prompt you to share information with a study partner and to search the Web for more information about famous castles around the world.

Famous castles around the world

ACTIVITY
2·1

Exchange experiences *Ask your partner the following questions, and add a question of your own.*

1. Which of the following castles and palaces are you familiar with? Indicate where each is located.

   ☐ Château de Versailles _____

   ☐ Schloss Schönbrunn _____

   ☐ Windsor Castle _____

   ☐ Castello di Strassoldo di Sopra _____

   ☐ Forbidden City _____

   ☐ Himeji Castle _____

   ☐ Rhodes Castle _____

   ☐ Krak des Chevalier _____

   ☐ Bran Castle _____

   ☐ Gyeongbok Palace _____

2. What do you think it would be like to live in a castle? What would be some of the advantages and disadvantages?

   _____

   _____

3. Your question _____

Discussion *Share your answers with another partner or with the whole group.*

ACTIVITY 2·2

Search the Web *Find information on famous castles around the world, and record the following details.*

Name of castle and location _____

URL www._____

Features and amenities _____

_____

_____

_____

_____

Name of castle and location _____

URL www._____

Features and amenities _____

_____

_____

_____

_____

Name of castle and location _____

URL www._____

Features and amenities _____

_____

_____

_____

_____

ACTIVITY 2·3

Writing *Describe the kind of castle you would build if you were King Ludwig II. Where would it be located, and what amenities would it have?*

The Three Racketeers
Wildlife experiences on a small island

Pre-reading

What are your favorite wild animals? Why?

- ☐ Bear
- ☐ Deer
- ☐ Elephant
- ☐ Giraffe
- ☐ Gorilla

- ☐ Hippopotamus
- ☐ Lion
- ☐ Monkey
- ☐ Tiger
- ☐ Wolf

☐ _____

☐ _____

Do you know any books, stories, or movies about unusual experiences with wild animals?

_____

Reading text

1   Scenic islands around the world attract dreamers who wish to flee the rat race of the city and live close to nature. The Southern Gulf Islands of British Columbia, Canada, are such a place, and Dee and Eric Hartley are two such people.

2   When the Hartleys decided to quit their jobs and change their lives, they sold their possessions and moved in August to a **rustic** half-acre property on Mayne Island on the west coast of British Columbia, Canada. Their new home was abundantly wooded with madrona, big-leaf maple, fir, and cedar trees, and a climb through the woods along deer trails and rocky terraces to the top of a bluff **terminated** in a wide-angle view of the Gulf Islands and Swanson Channel, with Vancouver Island and the Olympic Mountains of Washington State in the background. The couple was immediately sold on the view and the property's parklike setting. Here they felt sure they could lead a simple quiet life.

3   Although they had title to the land, the Hartleys soon discovered that they were not the only residents. Spiders scurried out of various hiding places and built their webs wherever they could be anchored. To avoid the afternoon sun, tree frogs climbed up to sit on the window ledges or the front awning of the Hartleys' aluminum travel trailer. A wire fence kept deer out of the yard, but they could be heard foraging in the surrounding woods. When a mouse came snooping around while the couple was having their lunch outside, they began to wonder who would show up next.

4   Early one December afternoon, a **sturdy** raccoon with a bushy, ringed tail sauntered across the snow-dusted yard and proceeded to climb a driftwood fence post. Like a clever acrobat, he straddled the roof of the bird feeder nailed to the gate and scooped out the birdseed with one hand while he clung to the feeder with the other. After a second attempt at night ended with the bird feeder in pieces on the ground, the Hartleys began leaving dinner leftovers outside in the hope that they could get a better look at their visitor, but he came around only occasionally at dusk. His thick, mottled gray, black-tipped fur **blended** so well with his surroundings that the Hartleys had to be **vigilant** to spot him. In February, scuffles, growls, yelps, and assorted noises at night **alerted** the Hartleys to courting combat in the woods. Twice, Bandit, as they named their visitor, showed up in the company of a female raccoon, but in spring he **resumed** his bachelor routine.

5   In March, a good-sized female turned up for a late brunch. Although from a distance she looked much like Bandit, she had a habit of attacking the food dish and running off with it into the woods. Not only did she have an **attitude**, but a nick in one ear and a missing toe on her left hind foot suggested that she had a history to match! The characteristic black mask across her face did nothing to hide the mischief in her black eyes, and with the slim, **agile** fingers of her silver-gloved hands she was able to grasp and grab whatever she fancied. In June, a younger female joined the crew. While she munched on her food, the newcomer liked to sit upright like a squirrel, and she often dipped her food or her hands in the water dish.

6   Bandit, Raggedy Ann, and Putzi generally traveled alone, but when one showed up, the next wasn't far behind. To prevent conflicts, the Hartleys scattered dry dog food on the ground instead of putting it in a dish. This **tactic** did not always work; when **inevitable** skirmishes broke out, the raccoons sorted things out in their own furious, but harmless, way. With the three raccoons coming to feed, squabble, and sometimes rest, the Hartleys' yard turned into a "garden stage." All they needed for the real show to begin was for Raggedy Ann or Putzi to show up with young. The Hartleys could hardly wait!

7   On the night of the summer solstice, the Hartleys were outside gazing at the stars when a strange warbling came from the woods. A couple of weeks later before suppertime, loud warbling and cooing sounds caught their attention again. Lined up on a big cedar log at the top of the yard were a trio of raccoon kits the size of kittens. The couple sat quietly on the bench outside, waiting for Raggedy Ann, but it was Putzi who appeared at the bottom. When she whistled, all three kits slid, tumbled, and bounced down the steep stone steps and landed in a furry **huddle**. At first, the kits scooted for cover and dived into the salal,[1] but at Putzi's signal they collected around her. The little raccoons could barely chew or swallow the big chunks of dog food, so they turned their investigations to the water container. Pulling themselves up onto the rim, they seesawed on the edge, and drank the water that dripped from their button-shaped noses.

8   The Hartleys had to wait until one lovely August afternoon for Putzi to bring her family again. A little later, Raggedy Ann, who disliked being upstaged, paraded across the garden stage with twins. Showtime had begun!

9   **Sporadic** at first, the raccoon family visits were more eventful than the national news on television. The kits enjoyed pulling on the bouncy red nicotiana flowers in the garden, or grappling with the ice plants as if they were knots that had to be untied. They fished among the various stones and rocks for goodies, and overturned an assortment of seashells to **check out** the underside. Empty flowerpots left on the stone steps became **irresistible** toys. Amazingly, Molly, Dolly, and Bugsy—Putzi's kits—never toppled tail over flowerpot onto the grass below.

---

[1] Salal is an evergreen, berry-producing shrub with leathery, glossy, dark green leaves; it is native to the Pacific Northwest region of North America.

10   Over the summer, the raccoons' education progressed to tree-climbing lessons. At first, the kits could scoot up a tree, but on their way down they slid and skittered until they could turn around and jump off. Once they'd mastered the art of climbing down headfirst like grown-up raccoons, they graduated from fir and cedar trees to the big arbutus, where they tussled in its crotch.

11   When the Three Racketeers,[2] as the bunch came to be known, raced through the herbs, knocked over a pot, dug a hole in the grass, or roughed up a plant, the Hartleys never regretted how quickly the raccoons had made themselves at home. If a plant or two fell victim to their play, the rare excitement of watching them learn and grow made up for any losses.[3]

Raccoon facts[4]

Scientific name	*Procyon lotor*
Geographical area	North America, but also found in Europe and Japan
Habitat	Woodland areas with evergreens and water; can be found in or near urban areas
Diet	Omnivore
Appearance	Grayish-brown fur
	A large bushy tail with 5 to 7 dark rings and a dark tip
	A mask across the face, with white bands above the eyes and around the nose
	Handlike front paws with elongated fingers and opposable thumbs; five toes with nonretractable claws
	Black ears with white tips
Average weight	Up to 10.4 kilograms; females are generally smaller than males
Length (including tail)	41 to 95 centimeters
Average life span	Up to 5 or 6 years in the wild; can live longer
Habits	Mostly nocturnal
Abilities	Highly developed sense of touch and keen vision
	Able to climb and swim
	Very adaptable and clever
Mating and breeding	January to June; kits are born in April and May
Size of litter	1 to 7 kits

---

[2] The name *Racketeers* is a play on words that combines *raccoon* and *Musketeer,* a group of three French swordsmen from Alexandre Dumas' classic novel *The Three Musketeers. Racketeers* also refers to criminals who make money from illegal activities, such as extortion or theft—two tricks at which raccoons are highly skilled.
[3] This story is adapted from the article "Encounters: The Three Racketeers" by D. S. Hartley, published in *Canadian Wildlife,* Vol. 14, No. 4, September–October 2008.
[4] From Erika Yery, "Raccoons—Facts and Fancies" (from *Rescue Report,* Wildlife Rescue League), http:// wildlife rescueleague.org/pdf/raccoon.pdf; and National Geographic Wild, http://animals.nationalgeographic .com/animals/mammals/raccoon/.

Vocabulary

EXERCISE
3·1

Organizing vocabulary *List the words and phrases from the reading text that relate to the following categories. An example has been provided for each category.*

1. Movement (verbs) (8) _scurry,_ _____

   _____

2. Conflict (nouns) (3) _scuffle,_ _____

3. Conflict (verbs) (3) _attack,_ _____

4. Eating (verbs) (5) _forage,_ _____

5. Animal noises (verbs and nouns) (5) _growl,_ _____

6. Arrival (verbs) (4) _show up,_ _____

7. Theater (verbs and nouns) (4) _upstage,_ _____

8. Nature (adjectives and nouns) (6) _rustic,_ _____

   _____

9. Observation (verbs) (3) _get a look at,_ _____

10. Group (nouns) (5) _crew,_ _____

Understanding vocabulary *Match each word or phrase in column 1 with its definition in column 2. Then, indicate each item's part of speech (n., v., or adj.).*

_____ 1. rustic _____
_____ 2. terminate _____
_____ 3. blend _____
_____ 4. sturdy _____
_____ 5. huddle _____
_____ 6. vigilant _____
_____ 7. tactic _____
_____ 8. inevitable _____
_____ 9. resume _____
_____ 10. attitude _____
_____ 11. check out _____
_____ 12. sporadic _____
_____ 13. alert _____
_____ 14. irresistible _____
_____ 15. agile _____

a. infrequent, irregular
b. watchful, observant
c. enchanting, overpowering
d. end in, finish
e. merge, mix in with
f. acrobatic, nimble
g. investigate, examine
h. simple, rural
i. unavoidable, unstoppable
j. warn, make aware
k. continue, carry on
l. strong, solid
m. bunch, cluster
n. strategy, method
o. demeanor, way of thinking

Using vocabulary *Complete each of the following sentences with the appropriate word from the list in Exercise 3-2. Be sure to use the correct form of each verb and to pluralize nouns, if necessary.*

1. Death is _____.

2. Red flashing lights _____ people to danger.

3. Our journey will _____ at Grand Central Station.

4. Gymnasts have to be very _____ in order to perform acrobatic feats and tricks.

5. Animals can hide easily, because their fur or skin _____ with their environment.

6. On our holiday in the mountains, we stayed overnight in a _____ log cabin.

7. When you are in a large crowd of people, you have to be _____ in case there are any pickpockets who will try to steal your wallet or purse.

8. After they paused to have lunch and fill the gas tank, the travelers _____ their journey.

9. Because the student's attendance at school was very _____, he missed a lot of important material and didn't pass his exams.

10. Children want to have a puppy or a kitten, because baby animals are so cute and

    _____.

11. When the children heard the thunder, they gathered in a tight _____ in the corner.

12. The chair fell apart when the man sat down, because it wasn't very _____ or well-made.

13. If you want to succeed in life, you need a positive _____.

14. Before you book your flight, you should _____ prices on the Internet.

15. To win the game, the players have to develop some clever _____.

Reading comprehension

Reading for main ideas *Answer each of the following questions with a complete sentence, using information from the reading text. Try not to copy directly from the text.*

1. Why did the Hartleys move to Mayne Island?

_____

2. How did they react to wild animals coming onto their property?

_____

3. What did the Hartleys think when the first raccoon appeared?

_____

4. How did all three raccoons behave when they ran into each other?

_____

5. Why did they think of their property as a "garden stage"?

_____

6. When did their most entertaining experience occur?

_____

7. What did the Hartleys enjoy most about having young raccoons come to visit?

_____

Reading for details *Indicate which of the following statements are true (T) and which are false (F).*

1. _____ Mayne Island is one of the Northern Gulf Islands of British Columbia, Canada.
2. _____ The Hartleys' property was like a park with lots of trees and wild animals.
3. _____ The Hartleys lived in a big house.
4. _____ At first, Bandit usually came when it was dark outside.
5. _____ The two raccoons who showed up after Bandit were females.
6. _____ The three raccoons traveled together and were very friendly toward each other.
7. _____ The raccoons had different habits and very different personalities.
8. _____ Raggedy Ann was the first female to bring her young.
9. _____ The Hartleys were able to observe five baby raccoons.
10. _____ The raccoons never did any serious damage to the Hartleys' property.

Reading for facts and figures *Using the information in the reading text and the chart of raccoon facts on page 24, complete the following sidebar to accompany a magazine article about raccoons.*

Did you know that . . .

raccoons have thick, mottled gray, black-tipped fur?

_____

_____

_____

_____

_____

_____

_____

_____

_____

_____

_____

_____

_____

Reading for meaning *For each of the following pairs of sentences, choose the boldface phrase in the second sentence that more closely matches the meaning of the underlined phrase in the first sentence, which is quoted from the reading text.*

1. "Scenic islands around the world attract dreamers who wish to flee <u>the rat race of the city</u> and live close to nature."

   People like the Hartleys move to small islands, because they don't like **the hectic pace of** | **the rats that run around in** the city.

2. "The couple <u>was</u> immediately <u>sold on</u> the view and the property's parklike setting."

   The Hartleys **bought** | **liked** the property right away.

3. "Although they <u>had title to</u> the land, the Hartleys soon discovered that they were not the only residents."

   The Hartleys **legally owned** | **gave a name to** the property on Mayne Island.

4. "In February, scuffles, growls, yelps, and assorted noises at night alerted the Hartleys to <u>courting combat</u> in the woods."

   The raccoons scuffled because they **were mating** | **were fighting over territory**.

5. "Not only did she have an attitude, but a nick in one ear and a missing toe on her left hind foot suggested that she <u>had a history</u> to match!"

   Raggedy Ann **was an older raccoon** | **looked like a fighter**.

6. "This tactic did not always work; when inevitable skirmishes broke out, the raccoons <u>sorted things out in their own furious, but harmless, way</u>."

   When they fought, the raccoons **harmed each other** | **didn't harm each other**.

7. "With the three raccoons coming to feed, squabble, and sometimes rest, the Hartleys' yard turned into a '<u>garden stage</u>'."

   The raccoons were **entertainers** | **a nuisance**.

8. "A little later, Raggedy Ann, who <u>disliked being upstaged</u>, paraded across the garden stage with twins."

   Raggedy Ann **didn't want to be Number One** | **wanted to be Number One**.

9. "Twice Bandit, as they named their visitor, showed up in the company of a female raccoon, but in spring he <u>resumed his bachelor routine</u>."

   Bandit liked to travel **alone** | **with another raccoon**.

10. "If a plant or two fell victim to their play, the rare excitement of watching them learn and grow <u>made up for any losses</u>."

    The Hartleys **minded** | **didn't mind** if the raccoons destroyed any of the plants in their garden.

Reading skills

Retelling the story *Imagine that you live on Mayne Island and are keeping a journal of your experiences. Make entries in the journal about your most important experiences. Don't copy from the reading text or invent details. The first entry has been provided.*

August 1995

A couple of weeks ago, we moved into our new home on Mayne Island, and we're very excited about living here. The property is peaceful, with different trees and a beautiful view from the top. We have lots of visitors: spiders, trees frogs, deer, and a mouse. I wonder who will show up next?

December 1995

_____

_____

_____

_____

_____

March 1996

_____

_____

_____

_____

_____

June 1996

_____

_____

_____

_____

_____

August 1996

_____

_____

_____

_____

_____

Web search and writing

The activities on the next two pages prompt you to share information with a study partner and to search the Web for more information about people's experiences with wildlife.

Wildlife experiences

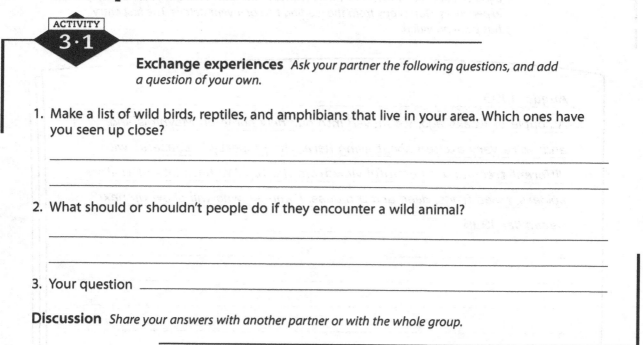

ACTIVITY 3·1

Exchange experiences *Ask your partner the following questions, and add a question of your own.*

1. Make a list of wild birds, reptiles, and amphibians that live in your area. Which ones have you seen up close?

_____

_____

2. What should or shouldn't people do if they encounter a wild animal?

_____

_____

3. Your question _____

Discussion *Share your answers with another partner or with the whole group.*

ACTIVITY 3·2

Search the Web *Find information about people's experiences with wild animals, and record the following details.*

Name of the animal _____

URL www._____

Details of the story _____

_____

_____

_____

Name of the animal   _____

URL   www._____

Details of the story   _____

_____

_____

_____

Name of the animal   _____

URL   www._____

Details of the story   _____

_____

_____

_____

_____

ACTIVITY
3·3

Writing *Write a list of actions that people and governments can take to protect wild animals and their habitat.*

The lure of lost treasure ships

Pre-reading

What stories can you imagine from the following headlines?

The Biggest Sunken Treasure Ever Found: $500 Million
Spanish Treasure Ship Missing Since 1681 Found
Sunken Treasure Ship Found 40 miles off Guyana's Coast
Divers Find £155m Silver Hoard on Wreck

If you found a lost treasure worth millions of dollars, what would you do?

_____

_____

Reading text

1   For anyone who has seen *Pirates of the Caribbean* or read Robert Louis Stevenson's *Treasure Island*, the **lure** of lost treasure ships **laden** with gold, silver, precious jewels, and priceless antiquities will take them back to the colonial period of the sixteenth and seventeenth centuries, when Spanish and Portuguese explorers conquered the Americas and sailed back to Europe with their bounty. If it's big treasure you're after, however, you might turn your attention to the lost treasure ships of the twentieth century. Between the two world wars, luxury liners, armored warships, merchant **vessels**, and freighters carried more than 700 tons of gold from war-torn Europe to safe havens in North America. Many, like the RMS *Titanic*, RMS *Lusitania*, and *HMS Edinburgh*, met with enemy attack or natural catastrophe and sank to the bottom of the sea. To this day, few treasure ships have ever been recovered.

2   Of the estimated three million shipwrecks scattered over the ocean floor, only the most commercially attractive ones have captured the attention of treasure hunters and salvors.[1] The most legendary is the *RMS Titanic*. On April 14, 1915, the 882-foot, 46,392-ton luxury liner **collided** with an iceberg and sank on its maiden voyage from Southampton, England, to New York City. Of the 2,223 people on board, 1,517 died in the tragedy. Lost but not forgotten, the *Titanic* and its treasures began to attract potential salvors in the 1960s, but it was not until the 1980s that Texas millionaire Jack Grimm undertook three separate expeditions, only to find no trace of the ship's **remains**.

_____

[1] *Salvors* are sailors and engineers who salvage ships.

3   On September 1, 1985, a French-American project located the *Titanic,* and in 1987, with the use of the submersible *Nautile,* salvors recovered an abundance of artifacts. A total of 5,500 objects were brought up from the **wreck**, including personal belongings of the passengers and crew, memorabilia, collectibles, porcelain, furniture, fixtures, ship parts, and **miscellaneous** articles of more value to historians, archaeologists, and museum visitors than to fortune seekers. *Titanic: The Artifact Exhibition,* the largest display of recovered artifacts from the ship, is on permanent display at the Luxor Hotel in Las Vegas, Nevada. In addition to more than 300 objects, the exhibit features stories of the passengers and a full-scale reproduction of the liner's Grand Staircase. Other expeditions, a few of which are listed in the table below, have been more rewarding than the discovery of the *Titanic.*

4   As adventuresome as it may seem, the hunt for treasure ships has always faced major challenges. Until the 1950s, treasure hunters had difficulty locating shipwrecks that lay thousands of meters deep in dark and dangerous waters. At the turn of the century, failure often resulted from the hit-and-miss process of dragging wire nets and lines from two or more ships across the seafloor until they caught on something. In 1918, the joint English-French Anti-Submarine Detection Investigation Committee (ASDIC) located enemy submarines by sending out sound pulses through the water. This revolutionary technique was used to locate the *Lusitania,* which sank off the coast of Ireland after a German U-boat attack on May 7, 1915. Echo-sounding **evolved** by the 1960s into sonar, which became a standard feature of marine navigation. In addition to side-scan sonar,[2] searchers can now employ sub-bottom profilers to image objects buried beneath layers of sediment. Modern satellite global positioning systems (GPS) can accurately determine the location of a lost ship in an area as small as 500 square miles.

5   Once a ship has been located, divers are sent to access the wreck, but their safety and success depend on suitable equipment. Pioneer divers had to wear heavy canvas suits, a copper helmet, lead boots weighing 40 pounds each, and lead weights of 16 pounds to **counteract** buoyancy. They could safely reach a maximum depth of only 200 feet. The time they could spend under water and the speed at which they could surface without suffering from the "bends"[3] were severely limited. In the 1940s, renowned French oceanographer Jacques Cousteau and associate Émile Gagnan developed the Aqua-Lung, or oxygen tank. This improvement in diver safety and mobility made diving more popular and treasure hunting more **feasible**.

6   Cousteau also contributed to the development of saturation diving, which allowed divers to live and work from a protected sea habitat. Using a small manned submarine called a submersible, divers are able to **withstand** external pressure at depths up to 20,000 feet and to work under water for up to three days. Originally developed for scientific and military purposes, submersibles are equipped with robotic arms to recover objects and to investigate areas of a wreck that would otherwise pose physical peril to divers.

7   Although advanced technology has made it easier for treasure hunters to find, access, investigate, and even raise sunken ships, there is no guarantee of success. A ship of interest can lie amid other wrecks, making it impossible to detect or distinguish. With the passage of time, sand and mud cover wreckage and the forces of nature **erode** and decompose steel, iron, wood, and other materials. Rugged, shifting terrain, as well as adverse marine and weather conditions, increase the risks of disaster to search crews.

8   The exact nature and value of a ship's cargo is often **subject to** a great deal of speculation. Since records were not always kept, particularly in wartime, the details of a ship's cargo could be

---

[2] Side-scan sonar maps the seafloor by emitting continuous sonar pulses while the investigating vessel is moving.
[3] The "bends" is a painful and potentially fatal condition that results when a diver who has been breathing compressed air rises too quickly to the surface; dissolved nitrogen forms bubbles in the bloodstream, producing the bends.

anybody's guess. Even if treasure hunters have deep-enough pockets and a broad time horizon to go on their quest, they have a good chance of ending up with no legal claim to their booty. Laws governing the ownership of shipwrecks and their contents and the right of salvage are complex, and no international agreements exist. Opponents of commercial salvage condemn these attempts as the **desecration** of graves, while some archaeologists argue that these sites should be preserved in their virgin state.

9   Despite the many obstacles, there are adventurers who cannot resist the lure of lost treasure. It is the sea, however, that remains in possession of these **doomed** vessels, and the sea is reluctant to give them up.

Notable discoveries and salvages

Ship	Date of wreck	Estimated treasure and/or value of cargo	Date of discovery/recovery
Mary Rose	1545	26,000 artifacts of historical and archaeological value	Discovered in 1971 by Alexander McKee; raised in 1982; museum opened in late 2012
Nuestra Señora de Atocha	1622	Copper, silver, gold, tobacco, gems, jewels, jewelry, and indigo	Discovered in 1985 by Mel Fisher after 16½ years of searching
Santa María de la Consolación	1681	Pieces of eight (coins) worth $20 to $100 million	Discovered in the mid-1990s by Roberto Aguirre
HMS *Sussex*	1694	Gold and silver coins worth $4 billion	Recently discovered
Admiral Nakhimov	May 28, 1905	British gold sovereigns, platinum and gold bars worth almost $3 billion	Recovered in 1980, after 50 years of fruitless effort
RMS *Lusitania*	May 7, 1915	Various artifacts; presence of gold and valuables still shrouded in mystery	First discovered in 1935; explored from the 1960s to the present
Laurentic	January 25, 1917	3,211 gold bars worth more than $404 million	Located shortly after sinking; last recovery efforts in 1931
HMS *Edinburgh*	May 2, 1942	465 gold bars worth more than $2.5 million	Designated a war grave in 1957; discovered in April 1981; first gold recovered in September 1981

Vocabulary

Organizing vocabulary *List the words and phrases from the reading text that relate to the following categories. An example has been provided for each category.*

1. Sea-going vessels (9) __ships,__ _____

_____

2. Valuable objects (9) __treasure,__ _____

_____

3. Danger (7) __tragedy,__ _____

_____

Understanding vocabulary *Choose two words or phrases from the following list as synonyms of each numbered item below.*

artifact	challenge	locate	recover
booty	collectibles	lure	renowned
bounty	detect	obstacle	rewarding
capture attention	disaster	peril	salvage
catastrophe	legendary	priceless	shipwreck

1. treasure _____ _____

2. find _____ _____

3. save _____ _____

4. valuable _____ _____

5. accident _____ _____

6. problem _____ _____

7. danger _____ _____

8. antique _____ _____

9. attract _____ _____

10. famous _____ _____

Understanding vocabulary *Indicate the part of speech (n., v., or adj.) of each word in the following list. Then, using a dictionary, indicate each word's definition.*

Word and part of speech   **Definition**

1. laden _____   _____

2. miscellaneous _____   _____

3. counteract _____   _____

4. erode _____   _____

5. doomed _____   _____

6. remains _____   _____

7. wreck _____   _____

8. lure _____   _____

9. evolve _____   _____

10. feasible _____   _____

11. withstand _____   _____

12. subject to _____   _____

13. collide _____   _____

14. desecration _____   _____

15. vessel _____   _____

Using vocabulary *Complete each of the following sentences with the appropriate word(s) from the list in Exercise 4-3. Be sure to use the correct form of each verb and to pluralize nouns, if necessary.*

1. All that could be found at the site of the airplane crash was the _____ of the dead passengers.

2. Over the past several decades, communication technology has _____ dramatically.

3. Due to harsh weather conditions, the mountain-climbing expedition was

   _____ to failure, and after five days the team had to return to the base camp.

4. It is not _____ for human beings to live on another planet.

5. At Christmastime, people arrive at their families' homes _____ with presents and goodies.

6. The buttes, pinnacles, and spires of Badlands National Park in South Dakota were formed

   over centuries, as wind and water _____ the sandstone.

7. Many people were killed when the train _____ with a truck crossing

   the tracks. Of course, the truck was a total _____.

8. Every student at the university is _____ the same rules and regulations during exams.

9. The navy has just bought several new _____ for its fleet.

10. If you don't know where to record these expenses in your budget, you can just enter them

    under "_____."

11. In college, we have to complete so many assignments that sometimes it's not easy

    to _____ all the pressure.

12. The invading army's destruction of historical and cultural monuments is considered

    an act of _____.

13. The government will introduce new laws to _____ the threat of a terrorist attack.

14. In 1849, the _____ of gold and striking it rich drew many prospectors and fortune seekers to California.

Reading comprehension

EXERCISE
4·5

Reading for main ideas *Match each of the headlines in column 2 with the corresponding paragraph of the reading text.*

_____ Paragraph 1
_____ Paragraph 2
_____ Paragraph 3
_____ Paragraph 4
_____ Paragraph 5
_____ Paragraph 6
_____ Paragraph 7
_____ Paragraph 8
_____ Paragraph 9

a. *Titanic Treasure Disappoints*
b. *Submersibles and Robot Technology Allow Access to Wrecks*
c. *Titanic Considered Most Famous Shipwreck*
d. *No Guarantee of Ownership for Treasure Hunters*
e. *Diver Safety Key to Lost Ship Recovery*
f. *Ocean Keeps Guard over Sunken Treasures*
g. *Treasure Hunters Encounter Obstacles Despite Technological Advances*
h. *Lost 20th-Century Ships Laden with Valuable Treasure*
i. *Modern Technology Improves Chances of Detection*

EXERCISE
4·6

Reading for details *Answer the following questions in your own words, using complete sentences.*

1. What makes the lost ships of the twentieth century so attractive to treasure hunters?

_____

2. How many lost ships are believed to lie at the bottom of the ocean?

_____

3. How has technology advanced to make locating lost treasure ships easier and more exact?

In the past _____

In the present _____

4. How has technology advanced to make diving safer?

In the past _____

In the present _____

5. What technological advances have made it easier to access and investigate lost treasure ships?

_____

6. What problems do salvors encounter even if they can recover a ship's treasure?

_____

_____

7. Why do some people think that lost ships should be left undisturbed?

_____

_____

EXERCISE
4·7

Reading for facts and figures *Using information in the table on page 36, choose answers to the questions below from the following list. Some answers are used more than once.*

a. *Mary Rose*
b. *Nuestra Señora de Atocha*
c. *Santa María de la Consolación*
d. HMS *Sussex*
e. *Admiral Nakhimov*
f. RMS *Lusitania*
g. *Laurentic*
h. HMS *Edinburgh*

1. Artifacts of which ship are on display in a museum? _____

2. Which ship was discovered recently? _____

3. Which ships sank during World War I? _____

4. Which ship sank during World War II? _____

5. The wreck of which ship was located shortly after sinking? _____

6. Which ship is believed to have been carrying gold and valuables? _____

7. The wrecks of which ships were located in the 1980s? _____

8. Which ships were carrying coins? _____

9. Which ships were carrying gold bars? _____

10. Which ships sank in the seventeenth century? _____

Reading for meaning *For each of the following statements, choose the answer that is closer in meaning.*

1. "If it's big treasure you're after, however, you might turn your attention to the lost treasure ships of the twentieth century."
   a. The cargo of sixteenth- and seventeenth-century Spanish and Portuguese ships is probably more valuable.
   b. The cargo of sixteenth- and seventeenth-century Spanish and Portuguese ships is probably less valuable.

2. "A total of 5,500 objects were brought up from the wreck [of the *Titanic*] . . . of more value to historians, archaeologists, and museum visitors than to fortune seekers."
   a. The treasure on the *Titanic* was more valuable than most people estimated.
   b. The treasure on the *Titanic* was less valuable than most people estimated.

3. "At the turn of the century, failure often resulted from the hit-and-miss process of dragging wire nets and lines from two or more ships across the seafloor until they caught on something."
   a. Earlier methods of locating ships were not very effective.
   b. Earlier methods of locating ships were very effective.

4. "Only ambitious entrepreneurs with deep pockets and a broad time horizon can afford to go in search of lost ships."
   a. You need a lot of time and money to search for lost ships.
   b. You don't need a lot of time or money to search for lost ships.

5. "Even if treasure hunters have deep-enough pockets and a broad time horizon to go on their quest, they have a good chance of ending up with no legal claim to their booty."
   a. The law supports people who find and recover lost ships.
   b. The law doesn't support people who find and recover lost ships.

6. "The details of a ship's cargo could be anybody's guess."
   a. People can't be sure of what the ship was carrying.
   b. People can be sure of what the ship was carrying.

Reading skills

Outline *To summarize the main difficulties treasure hunters face, list supporting details from the reading text. Then, add your own thoughts on the subject.*

Locating a lost ship

    Depth _____

    Terrain _____

    Detection _____

Accessing a lost ship

    Dangers to divers _____

    Time needed to investigate _____

    Weather conditions _____

Financial obstacles

    Money needed _____

    Value of the cargo _____

Legal and ethical issues

    Legal ownership _____

    International agreements _____

    Gravesites _____

What additional difficulties and challenges can you think of?

_____

_____

_____

Web search and writing

As you can see from the table of notable discoveries and recoveries, there are millions of dollars in treasure lying at the bottom of the ocean. The activities on the next two pages prompt you to share information with a study partner and to search the Web for information about lost treasure ships.

Famous lost treasure ships

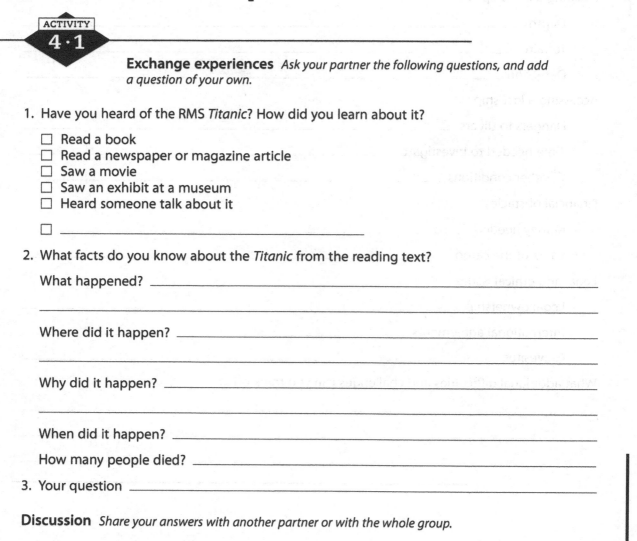

ACTIVITY 4·1

Exchange experiences *Ask your partner the following questions, and add a question of your own.*

1. Have you heard of the RMS *Titanic*? How did you learn about it?

   ☐ Read a book
   ☐ Read a newspaper or magazine article
   ☐ Saw a movie
   ☐ Saw an exhibit at a museum
   ☐ Heard someone talk about it

   ☐ _____

2. What facts do you know about the *Titanic* from the reading text?

   What happened? _____

   _____

   Where did it happen? _____

   _____

   Why did it happen? _____

   _____

   When did it happen? _____

   How many people died? _____

3. Your question _____

Discussion *Share your answers with another partner or with the whole group.*

ACTIVITY 4·2

Search the Web *Find information about other famous sunken ships and their treasures, and record the following details.*

Name of ship _____

URL www._____

Cause of wreck _____

_____

Treasure on board _____

Name of ship _____

URL www._____

Cause of wreck _____

_____

Treasure on board _____

Name of ship _____

URL www._____

Cause of wreck _____

_____

Treasure on board _____

ACTIVITY 4·3

Writing *Using the information that you found on the Web, imagine that you are a newspaper reporter and write a story about how a ship sank and what treasure it was carrying.*

Terry Fox
A real-life hero

Pre-reading

Do you know any real-life heroes? _____

What actions turn ordinary people into heroes?

☐ Saving a person's life
☐ Rescuing a child or animal in trouble
☐ Helping a disabled person
☐ Finding and returning someone else's valuable possession
☐ Preventing or stopping a crime
☐ Doing volunteer work
☐ Raising money for a good cause
☐ Overcoming difficulty or hardship

☐ _____

☐ _____

Reading text

1   At Mile Zero, the western starting point of Canada's Number 1 Highway in Victoria, British Columbia, there stands a life-size bronze statue of a young, curly-headed long-distance runner. He is wearing a **prosthetic** limb where his right leg had been, and the expression on his face is a mixture of pain, exhaustion, and sheer **determination**. He has cancer and he is running against time. The young man's name is Terry Fox.

2   Terry Stanley Fox was born on July 28, 1958, and grew up in Port Coquitlam, British Columbia. Throughout his school years, he was active in sports. He loved basketball, and although he was too short to qualify for the school team in Grade 8, hard work and **persistence** earned him a place the following year. In Grade 12, he and his best friend received their high school's **Athlete** of the Year award. Terry wanted to become a Physical Education teacher, and after graduating from high school in 1977, he began studying kinesiology[1] at Simon Fraser University in Burnaby.

3   In December 1976, Terry experienced sharp pain in his right knee. By March of the following year, the pain had become so severe that he went to the hospital, where he was **diagnosed** with osteosarcoma. This **aggressive** form of bone **cancer**

_____

[1] Kinesiology is the study of the mechanics of body movement.

is the sixth most common cancer among children; it particularly afflicts teenage boys. Terry's right leg was **amputated** 15 centimeters above the knee, and he underwent chemotherapy. Doctors gave him a 50 percent chance of **survival**.

4   After treatment, Terry made rapid progress as a result of his positive thinking and the same determination that had served him in school. Three weeks after the amputation, he was walking with a prosthetic limb and playing golf with his father. His experiences during the 16 months at the British Columbia Cancer Control Agency facility, however, left their mark on Terry. Watching other young cancer patients suffer and die awakened a deep **compassion** in him, and he made it his personal mission to raise **awareness** and funds for cancer research.

5   **Inspired** by the story of an amputee who ran in the New York City Marathon, Terry decided to undertake his own cross-Canada marathon. His goal was to raise $24 million, one dollar for every Canadian. He trained for 15 months—in itself, no small feat. To adjust to his artificial leg, he developed a hop-step gait that was to become his trademark. The **strain** on both his good leg and the stump of his right leg caused bruises, blisters, and intense pain, which he was able to overcome after 20 minutes or so of running. In August 1979, Terry ran his first marathon in Prince George, British Columbia; he came in last, but his spirit was undefeated.

6   In October 1979, Terry appealed to the Canadian Cancer Society for their support in his cross-country quest. In his letter, he wrote the following.

> We need your help. The people in cancer clinics all over the world need people who believe in miracles. I am not a dreamer, and I am not saying that this [marathon] will initiate any kind of definitive answer or cure to cancer. I believe in miracles. I have to.[2]

In addition to writing to corporations for **donations** to cover his expenses, vehicle costs, and gear, Terry requested government grants to pay for an artificial limb that he could run on. With financial support in place and a go-ahead from his doctors, Terry set out on April 12, 1980, from the east coast at St. Johns, Newfoundland. He began by dipping his leg in the Atlantic Ocean and filling two bottles with ocean water. When he reached Vancouver on the west coast, he planned to dip his leg again and pour one of the bottles into the Pacific Ocean. The cards seemed stacked against Terry. In the first days of his run, he encountered gale-force winds, heavy rain, and snowstorms. Later, in the peak of summer, he ran in extreme heat and humidity. His course followed the Trans-Canada highway, where drivers were not always respectful of Terry and his team. Running 42 kilometers a day took an immense toll on his body, but despite shin splints, an inflamed knee, cysts on his stump, dizzy spells, and tendonitis, Terry continued.

7   The strenuous days through Newfoundland, Nova Scotia, Prince Edward Island, New Brunswick, Quebec, and Ontario were not without their highlights. Terry was disappointed with poor public reception at first, but his courage and doggedness eventually attracted the attention of celebrities and the media. Upon learning about Terry, the founder of the Four Seasons Hotels and Resorts, whose son had died of melanoma, provided the team with accommodation and food, pledged two dollars for every mile run, and rallied other corporations to Terry's cause. By the time Terry reached Montreal on June 22, he had collected $200,000. On July 1, he arrived in Ottawa for the Canada Day celebrations and performed the ceremonial kickoff at a Canadian Football League game to a standing ovation. Along the way, he was joined by National Hockey League heroes who presented him with checks. Tireless and undaunted, Terry spoke at functions and events arranged by the Canadian Cancer Society. His name soon became a household word in Canada.

8   On September 1, 1980—143 days after he began his run—a coughing fit, chest pains, and shortness of breath forced Terry to stop outside Thunder Bay, Ontario; he entered the hospital.

---

[2] Terry's letter to the Canadian Cancer Society, posted on http://www.terryfox.org.

The cancer, he announced at a press conference, had spread to his lungs. A few days after he was **hospitalized**, television broadcaster CTV held a five-hour nationwide telethon with Canadian and international celebrities, adding $10 million to the $1.7 million Terry had already raised. With 5,373 kilometers behind him and 3,108 to go, Terry hoped to beat the cancer and continue his run. On June 28, 1981, one month before his twenty-third birthday, Terry Fox lost his battle with cancer. In the eyes of Canadians, Terry died a hero.

9   To this day, Terry Fox has not been forgotten. Organizations and events all over the world have raised more than $600 million in his honor. Launched in 1981, the Terry Fox Run takes place every September on the second Sunday after Labor Day in communities large and small, all across Canada. Supported by the Terry Fox Foundation, the event is organized and run by volunteers and is open to everyone. Terry Fox lives on as a symbol of courage and as an inspiration to do good in the world. The many statutes and monuments, buildings and organizations that bear Terry's name are enduring reminders of what one person can achieve when he puts his heart and mind to a task.

Tributes and honors to Terry Fox[3]

September 18, 1980	Youngest recipient of the Companion of the Order of Canada
November 22, 1980	Received the Sword of Hope, the American Cancer Society's highest honor
December 18, 1980	Received the Lou Marsh Award for outstanding athletic accomplishment
December 23, 1980	Voted Canadian press's Canadian of the Year; honored again in 1981
June 6, 1981	Simon Fraser University awarded the first Terry Fox Medal, given annually to a student who demonstrates courage in the face of adversity
July 17, 1981	Mount Terry Fox named in the Rocky Mountains
July 30, 1981	An 83-kilometer section of the Trans-Canada Highway named Terry Fox Courage Highway
	Terry Fox Humanitarian Award created; a $5 million endowment fund created to provide scholarships to students who demonstrate humanitarian service as well as academic excellence
August 29, 1981	Inducted posthumously into the Canadian Sports Hall of Fame with a permanent exhibit
September 1981	First annual Terry Fox Run
October 21, 1981	A Terry Fox stamp issued by Canada Post
April 13, 1982	Named to the Order of the Dogwood, British Columbia
June 26, 1982	2.7-meter bronze statue unveiled at Terry Fox Lookout, Thunder Bay, Ontario
May 26, 1988	Terry Fox Foundation became an independent trust
February 11, 1994	Terry Fox Hall of Fame created to recognize Canadians who have assisted disabled people
June 30, 1999	Voted Canada's greatest hero in a national survey
July 1, 1999	Monument in Ottawa rededicated as part of the Path of Heroes

---

[3] From http://www.terryfox.org.

January 17, 2000	A second stamp issued as part of Canada Post's Millennium Collection of influential and distinguished Canadians
January 27, 2003	Included in *Time* magazine's feature story, "Canada's Best"
March 14, 2005	First Canadian citizen commemorated on a one-dollar coin
April 12, 2005	Monument unveiled in St. Johns, Newfoundland
	Terry, a pictorial book by Douglas Coupland, became a No. 1 bestseller
September 9, 2005	Statue unveiled at Terry Fox Secondary School in Port Coquitlam, British Columbia
September 16, 2005	Statue unveiled at Mile Zero in Victoria, British Columbia, and three million students take part in Terry Fox National School Run Day
September 18, 2005	Statue unveiled in Prince George, British Columbia
October 29, 2007	Terry Fox Research Institute launched to gather clinical knowledge and scientific research
September 16, 2011	A series of four bronze statues unveiled at BC Place in Vancouver

In addition to the awards and honors listed here, 14 schools, 15 roads, numerous streets, libraries, and scholarship programs are named for Terry Fox. Several books have been written, and movies and videos produced, about his life and his Marathon of Hope.

Vocabulary

EXERCISE 5·1

Organizing vocabulary *Choose the words and phrases from the reading text that relate to the following categories. An example has been provided for each category.*

1. Medical procedures (6) _diagnose,_ _____

_____

2. Medical problems/conditions (15) _cancer,_ _____

_____

_____

3. A strong will (7) _determination,_ _____

_____

4. Sports (6) _basketball,_ _____

_____

5. Weather conditions (4) _gale-force winds,_ _____

_____

Understanding vocabulary *Complete the following chart with the correct forms of the words from the reading text. Using a dictionary, indicate the definition of each word.*

Noun	Adjective	Verb	Definition
1. _____		diagnose	_____
2. determination	_____	_____	_____
3. _____		inspire	_____
4. persistence	_____	_____	_____
5. strain	_____	_____	_____
6. survival	_____	_____	_____
7. _____	X	amputate	_____
8. donation	X	_____	_____
9. _____	X	hospitalize	_____
10. _____	prosthetic	X	_____
11. athlete	_____	X	_____
12. _____	aggressive	X	_____
13. compassion	_____	X	_____
14. awareness	_____	X	_____
15. cancer	_____	X	_____

EXERCISE
5·3

Understanding vocabulary *Match each of the following definitions with the corresponding underlined idiom in the numbered items below.*

a. When nothing is in a person's favor.
b. When a person decides to accomplish something no matter what happens.
c. When a person has very little time to do something.
d. When everyone knows who a person is and talks about him.
e. When something makes a deep impression on a person.
f. When something is very hard on a person's physical or mental well-being.
g. When someone gets other people to support something important.

_____ 1. "He <u>is running against time</u>."

_____ 2. "His experiences during the 16 months at the British Columbia Cancer Control Agency facility, however, <u>left their mark</u> on Terry."

_____ 3. "The cards seemed <u>stacked against</u> Terry."

_____ 4. "Running 42 kilometers a day <u>took an immense toll on</u> his body."

_____ 5. "His name soon became <u>a household word</u> in Canada."

_____ 6. "The founder of the Four Seasons Hotels and Resorts . . . <u>rallied</u> other corporations to Terry's cause."

_____ 7. "The many statutes and monuments, buildings and organizations that bear Terry's name are enduring reminders of what one person can achieve <u>when he puts his heart and mind to</u> a task."

EXERCISE
5·4

Using vocabulary *Complete each of the following sentences with the appropriate word(s) from the chart in Exercise 5-2. Be sure to use the correct form of each verb and to pluralize nouns, if necessary.*

1. Around Christmastime, many charitable organizations ask people for

   _____.

2. After the patient was _____ with tuberculosis, he was

   _____ for treatment.

3. Smoking can cause lung _____.

4. In order to reach your goals in life, you need _____ and

   _____.

5. International _____ compete every four years in the Olympic Games.

6. We should always show _____ for people who are less fortunate.

7. I was deeply _____ when I listened to Martin Luther King, Jr.'s "I Have a Dream" speech.

8. There are many public service announcements designed to raise teenagers' _____ of the dangers of binge drinking.

9. If you're not careful when you lift heavy objects, you can easily _____ your back muscles.

10. Nowadays, thanks to medical technology, people who have had to undergo an _____ can be fitted with a _____ device that allows them to regain normal function of their lost limb.

11. Some forms of cancer are more _____ than others and have to be detected early in order for the patient to _____.

Reading comprehension

EXERCISE
5·5

Reading for main ideas *Rewrite the following sentences, correcting the errors.*

1. Terry Fox became active in sports after he graduated from high school, because he was afraid to try out for team sports.

_____

_____

2. After Terry was diagnosed with bone cancer, the doctors said that he had a very good chance for complete recovery.

_____

_____

3. Terry recovered quickly from his operation because he was lucky.

_____

4. Terry was not affected by the other patients at the British Columbia Cancer Control Agency facility.

_____

_____

5. Terry decided to run a marathon across Canada, because he wanted to be the first amputee to set a record.

_____

_____

6. When Terry started out, he received instant support from the public.

_____

7. Terry had to discontinue his run because he ran out of financing.

_____

8. When Terry found out that the cancer had spread to his lungs, he decided to give up his quest.

_____

_____

9. Events to raise money in Terry Fox's name take place in Canada only.

_____

10. Not many people have heard of Terry Fox.

_____

EXERCISE
5·6

Reading for details *Fill in the blanks with details from the reading text.*

1. Terry lost his _____ leg to _____ cancer

   at the age of _____.

2. Terry wanted to become a _____, and he began to study

   _____ at Simon Fraser University.

3. After his operation, Terry was able to walk with a(n) _____.

4. _____ inspired Terry to run a _____ across

   Canada. His goal was to raise _____ for _____.

5. Terry wrote to _____, _____, and

   _____ for financial support for _____,

   _____, _____, and a(n) _____.

6. Terry began his run in _____ and planned to finish it in

   _____.

7. Terry ran _____ kilometers a day and completed a total of

   _____ kilometers. He had to stop outside _____

   on _____.

8. Terry raised a total of _____, but he died on _____

   at the age of _____.

9. So far, organizations have raised more than _____ in Terry's honor.

10. The _____ was launched in _____, and takes

   place every year in _____.

Reading for facts and figures *Answer the following questions, using information from the chart on pages 48–49.*

1. How many statues were unveiled at BC Place in Vancouver? _____

2. Who can receive the Terry Fox Humanitarian Award? _____

3. In which mountain range is a peak named for Terry Fox? _____

4. Which magazine included Terry Fox's story in a feature entitled "Canada's Best"?

   _____

5. How long is the Terry Fox Courage Highway? _____

6. When was the first annual Terry Fox Run held? _____

7. When was Terry named a Companion of the Order of Canada? _____

8. How many stamps have been issued in Terry's honor? _____

9. When was a coin issued to commemorate Terry? _____

10. In which Canadian cities can you find statues of Terry Fox or monuments to his memory?

    _____

Reading for meaning *For each of the following statements, quoted from the reading text, choose the answer that is closer in meaning.*

1. "Three weeks after the amputation, he was walking with a prosthetic limb and playing golf with his father."
   a. Terry's illness was not so serious because he was soon walking and playing golf.
   b. Terry soon walked and played golf despite the seriousness of his illness.

2. "Watching other young cancer patients suffer and die awakened a deep compassion in him, and he made it his personal mission to raise awareness and funds for cancer research."
   a. Terry believed that he could do something to help young cancer patients.
   b. Terry believed that he couldn't do anything to help young cancer patients.

3. "He trained for 15 months—in itself, no small feat."
   a. Terry's training wasn't very difficult.
   b. Terry's training was very difficult.

4. "I am not a dreamer, and I am not saying that this [marathon] will initiate any kind of definitive answer or cure to cancer."
   a. Terry expected his run to completely succeed.
   b. Terry didn't expect his run to completely succeed.

5. "I believe in miracles. I have to."
   a. Terry thought that only a miracle could cure him.
   b. Terry thought that a miracle couldn't cure him.

Reading skills

Profile of a real-life hero *The Oxford Dictionary defines a hero as "a person who is admired for courage, outstanding achievement, or noble qualities." Summarize the characteristics that make Terry Fox a hero. Support your points with examples from the reading text. The first characteristic and one example are provided.*

1. _determination_

   When Terry's cancer spread to his lungs, he still planned to beat the cancer

   and continue his run.

2. _____

   _____

   _____

3. _____

   _____

   _____

4. _____

   _____

   _____

5. _____

   _____

   _____

6. _____

   _____

   _____

7. _____

   _____

   _____

Web search and writing

The activities on the next two pages prompt you to share information with a study partner and to search the Web for more information about real-life heroes.

Real-life heroes

ACTIVITY 5·1

Exchange experiences *Ask your partner the following questions, and add a question of your own.*

1. What characteristics do you think heroes possess?

   ☐ Courage   ☐ Kindness
   ☐ Determination   ☐ Physical strength
   ☐ Generosity   ☐ Self-confidence
   ☐ Humility   ☐ Self-sacrifice

   ☐ _____   ☐ _____

2. What causes do you think people should support or volunteer for? What do you do to help people who are sick, poor, or less fortunate than you?

   _____

   _____

3. Your question _____

Discussion *Share your answers with another partner or with the whole group.*

ACTIVITY 5·2

Search the Web *Find information about real-life heroes, and record the following details.*

Name of person   _____

URL   www._____

His or her achievements   _____

_____

_____

_____

_____

Name of person   _____

URL   www._____

His or her achievements   _____

_____

_____

_____

_____

Name of person   _____

URL   www._____

His or her achievements   _____

_____

_____

_____

_____

ACTIVITY
5·3

Writing *Choose one of these real-life heroes and write a list of questions you would like to ask if you had the chance to interview him or her.*

Storm chasers
Scientists, nature freaks, or daredevils?

Pre-reading

Name 10 kinds of weather conditions or weather phenomena.

1. _____ 6. _____

2. _____ 7. _____

3. _____ 8. _____

4. _____ 9. _____

5. _____ 10. _____

Have you ever experienced an extreme weather event? If so, describe it.

_____

_____

Reading text

1   We have all seen the pictures on the news: crumpled trailers, flattened houses, uprooted trees, overturned cars, shattered glass, twisted metal, downed power lines, toppled telephone poles, collapsed bridges, flooded fields and neighborhoods, **debris** and wreckage scattered for miles in the wake of a raging tornado or hurricane. Losing a loved one, or everything one owns, to a natural disaster is everyone's worst nightmare. So, why would anyone in his right mind want to risk his life chasing after the kind of weather most people pray will never come their way?

2   There have always been people who like to observe and **track** the weather, but the pastime or passion of storm chasing got its start in the mid-1950s, when researchers and government employees went out into the field to gather scientific information about severe weather events. In order to improve weather forecasting and safety, the National Severe Storms Laboratory (NSSL) was set up in 1964 in Oklahoma, part of Tornado Alley, where 90 percent of all tornadoes in the United States touch down. In 1972, the University of Oklahoma developed the Tornado Intercept Project and engaged meteorology students to **intercept**, film, and photograph tornadoes. By the 1990s, Doppler radar and advanced weather tracking technology had enabled researchers to collect data, and government-sponsored programs like VORTEX (Verification of Origins of Rotation in Tornadoes Experi-

ment) improved understanding of how tornadoes develop, as well as the ability to **forecast** when and where they would strike.

3   Although tornadoes in the United States begin with a gentle southern breeze coming off the Gulf of Mexico, the forces of nature can turn them into devils. As warm moist air flows toward the Great Plains, it mixes with hot dry air from the American South and cold air moving down from the Canadian Arctic. Together, the hot air and cold air force the tropical air to rise rapidly, creating an updraft that sucks **condensation** into the atmosphere. This moisture climbs tens of thousands of feet, forming a huge cumulonimbus cloud. At the base of the cloud, winds blow from different directions at varying speeds and **elevations**, and **exert** forces on the **saturated** air inside the cloud until the air begins to spin in a clockwise direction. At the top of the cloud, cooling moisture turns to ice crystals, and the entire structure—called a supercell thunderstorm—lets loose with thunder, lightning, torrential rain, and, at times, hailstones as big as baseballs.

4   Tornadoes are unpredictable in size, shape, and behavior. They can be 300 feet to two miles wide, spin at 261 to 381 miles per hour, and last for minutes or hours. Heads of tornadoes can be shaped like pancakes, anvils, or wedges with long, straight or bent tails that **resemble** ropes, drill bits, stovepipes, elephant trunks, or cones. They can be black or white, or take on the color of the soil that whirls up off the ground. They can occur singly or in deadly sequence. They can turn cars into missiles and other objects into projectiles. They can injure, maim, and kill. They can wipe an entire town off the map and cause billions of dollars of damage. In Tornado Alley, tornado season lasts from early spring to fall, with a brief pause in late spring and early summer.

5   Whereas tornadoes form over land, hurricanes are born over water. From summer to fall, hurricanes—also called typhoons or tropical cyclones—form when hot air, often from the Sahara Desert, races over the Atlantic Ocean. As these columns of hot air spin, they pick up moisture and attract strong winds that bend as the storm travels. At the center of the rotating storm is the eye, a **deceptively** calm area of low pressure that can stretch from two to 200 miles in diameter. **Encircling** the eye is the eye wall, the most intense part of the storm. Most hurricanes die at sea, but if sufficiently **fueled** with moisture and driven by tremendous winds, all hell breaks loose when they hit land. In August 2005, Hurricane Katrina, the worst Atlantic hurricane on record, roared from the Bahamas toward Louisiana with winds up to 175 miles per hour and laid waste to the city of New Orleans. More than 1,800 people were killed, and property damage was estimated at more than $81 billion.

6   Over the past 20 years, extreme weather has become a media **spectacle**. In 1992, Senator Al Gore (later vice president of the United States) introduced the concept of global warming[1] in *Earth in the Balance: Ecology and the Human Spirit*. Gore's book echoed professors, NASA scientists, and meteorological researchers who had already warned of climate change and **predicted** more frequent and disastrous hurricanes, drought, and floods in the future. In the 1990s, weather was making the news on the Weather Channel, and by 2001, 80 million US households were tuning in to watch dramatic footage of weather-related catastrophes. When *Twister*, the second-highest grossing film of 1996, featured a glamorous team of researchers competing to **deploy** a data-gathering device inside a tornado, a new breed of weather fanatics, nature freaks, entrepreneurs, and adrenaline addicts with laptops and cell phones hit the road in hot pursuit. By selling live footage to sensation-hungry television stations, a daring storm chaser could make a name for himself and money to finance the next chase. Videos were popping up on YouTube, and in October 2007, the Discovery Channel premiered *Storm Chasers*, a popular documentary reality series that ran until January 2012.

---

[1] The critically acclaimed documentary film *An Inconvenient Truth* in 2006 popularized the issue of global warming. Al Gore and the U.N.'s Intergovernmental Panel on Climate Change (IPCC) received the Nobel Peace Prize in 2007.

7   Storm chasing is not for the faint of heart. For serious storm chasers, getting up close and personal with an F4 tornado on the Fujita Scale[2] is about science and safety. For newcomers, it's the thrill of the hunt, and for journalists and videographers, it's about being the first to capture the event on camera. Without the proper equipment, knowledge, and experience, every storm chaser, whether motivated by science or adventure, is at the mercy of Mother Nature. So far, no deaths have been reported among storm chasers, but some have been struck by lightning, and many have been scared out of their wits. Despite the risks, the number of storm chasers is growing. In 2011, there were 1,690 tornadoes in the United States and a record 350 storm chasers registered for Chaser Con, the National Storm Chaser Convention in Denver, Colorado.

8   According to a 2010 World Meteorological Organization study, one-third fewer hurricanes have been predicted. However, their wind speeds are expected to increase by 100 percent and cause 60 percent more damage. As the climate warms, convective storms will intensify, which translates into mightier Hurricane Katrinas. So, the next time you hear of a storm coming, you can grab your camera, hop in the car, and hit the gas—or more wisely, run for cover and hope the storm won't be as bad as the weather forecaster says.

---

[2] The Fujita Scale was created by and named for Tetsuya Fujita, a University of Chicago meteorologist, in 1971 and modified in 2007 into the Enhanced Fujita Scale. According to the scale, tornadoes are classified as follows: F0 (under 73 mph), F1 (73–112 mph), F2 (113–157 mph), F3 (158–206 mph), and F4 (207–260 mph). Hurricanes are measured by the Saffir-Simpson Hurricane Scale, which specifies five categories of wind speed, ranging in strength from 74 mph to over 150 mph.

Vocabulary

EXERCISE
6·1

Organizing vocabulary *List the words and phrases from the reading text that relate to the following headings. Add the part of speech or grammatical element (n., v., adj., or id. for idiom) for each word or phrase. An example has been provided for each heading.*

Natural disasters	Weather and meteorology	Damage and destruction
tornado (n.)	*thunder (n./v.)*	*crumpled (adj.)*

Understanding and using vocabulary *Complete the following chart with the correct forms of the words from the reading text.*

	Noun	Verb	Adjective/adverb
1.	_____	_____	saturated
2.	_____	_____	deceptive(ly)
3.	_____	predict	_____
4.	_____	deploy	_____
5.	elevation	_____	_____
6.	_____	encircle	X
7.	_____	fuel	X
8.	_____	forecast	X
9.	_____	intercept	X
10.	condensation	_____	X
11.	_____	track	X
12.	_____	exert	X
13.	_____	resemble	X
14.	spectacle	X	X
15.	debris	X	X

Understanding and using vocabulary *For each of the following statements, choose the appropriate word or phrase from the chart in Exercise 6-2 as a replacement for the underlined word or phrase. Be sure to use the correct form of each verb and to pluralize nouns, if necessary.*

1. The weatherman <u>has predicted</u> scattered thunderstorms for the weekend.

   _____

2. The mass media has the power to <u>strengthen</u> debate on controversial issues.

   _____

3. When we got caught in the rainstorm, our clothes got <u>completely soaked with water</u>.

   _____

4. Before the police could enter the building, they had to <u>apply</u> a lot of force to break down the door.

   _____

5. After Hurricane Katrina struck New Orleans, the city and the misery of its victims became a media <u>show of enormous proportions</u>.

   _____

6. After the tsunami, all that was left of the houses lining the shore was <u>scattered fragments</u>.

   _____

7. Meteorologists use Doppler radar to <u>follow the movement of</u> approaching storms.

   _____

8. The rock star was <u>surrounded</u> by fans before he could enter the stadium.

   _____

9. In this photograph, I <u>look like</u> my mother when she was my age.

   _____

10. When the weather is cold, steam from boiling water in the kitchen forms <u>water droplets that collect</u> on the inside of the windows.

    _____

11. A salesman can be <u>misleadingly</u> friendly to people when he wants to sell them something they don't need.

    _____

12. The weather on the West Coast can be difficult to <u>estimate in advance</u>. One minute, it's nice and sunny, and the next, it can start to rain.

    _____

13. Two policemen <u>blocked and seized</u> the robbers as they fled from the jewelry store.

    _____

14. Just before the airplane hit the water, the pilot <u>brought into service</u> the emergency landing gear.

    _____

15. When mountain climbers reach higher <u>heights above sea level</u>, they have difficulty breathing because of the decreased oxygen in the air.

    _____

Understanding and using vocabulary *For each of the following statements, choose the answer that is closer in meaning to the underlined idiom.*

1. "So, why would anyone <u>in his right mind</u> want to risk his life chasing after the kind of weather most people pray will never come their way?"
   a. sane
   b. correct

2. "Most hurricanes die at sea, but if sufficiently fueled with moisture and driven by tremendous winds, <u>all hell breaks loose</u> when they hit land."
   a. hurricanes break up
   b. hurricanes become very destructive

3. "Storm chasing is <u>not for the faint of heart</u>."
   a. not for people with heart disease
   b. not for people who become easily afraid

4. "For serious storm chasers, <u>getting up close and personal</u> with an F4 tornado on the Fujita Scale is about science and safety."
   a. making very close contact
   b. making friends

5. "Without the proper equipment, knowledge, and experience, every storm chaser, whether motivated by science or adventure, <u>is at the mercy of Mother Nature</u>."
   a. is completely dependent on nature
   b. is grateful to nature

Reading comprehension

EXERCISE
6·5

Reading for main ideas *One way to determine the main idea in a piece of text is to find the topic sentence. Each paragraph contains a topic sentence that determines the subject matter of the paragraph; the first sentence of a paragraph is often its topic sentence. Find the topic sentence in each paragraph of the reading text and paraphrase it below.*

Paragraph 1 _____

_____

Paragraph 2 _____

_____

Paragraph 3 _____

_____

Paragraph 4 _____

_____

Paragraph 5 _____

_____

Paragraph 6 _____

_____

Paragraph 7 _____

_____

Paragraph 8 _____

_____

Reading for details *Add details from the reading text to the following outline about tornadoes.*

1. Size _____

2. Shape

    Head _____

    Tail _____

3. Color _____

4. Frequency _____

5. Speed of travel _____

6. Tornado season _____

7. Effects on humans and property

    _____

    _____

    _____

    _____

8. Formation of tornadoes

    Moist air _____

    The hot and cold air _____

    Condensation _____

    Winds _____

    Moisture at the top _____

    The result _____

9. Difference between a tornado and a hurricane

    _____

    _____

Reading for facts and figures *Complete the following sentences with dates and figures from the reading text.*

1. In _____, Hurricane Katrina destroyed most of the city of

   _____, killed _____ people, and caused property

   damage estimated at more than _____.

2. _____ percent of all storms in the United States occur in the area known

   as _____.

3. By 2001, _____ households in the United States were watching the
   Weather Channel.

4. In 2011, there were _____ tornadoes in the United States.

5. A World Meteorological Organization study in _____ predicted that

   hurricanes will decrease in number by _____, but will cause

   _____ percent more damage.

6. The eye of a hurricane can measure _____ in diameter.

7. The NSSL (_____) was established in _____.

Reading for meaning *Using information from the reading text, indicate which of the following actions people should, and should not, do when they chase storms.*

1. Make an exit plan; know how to get to safety.

2. Drive into the storm and get as close as you can to the eye.

3. Respect the privacy of victims and their property.

4. Be prepared; make sure your car has a full tank of gas, and assemble food, water, a first-aid kit, and emergency equipment and supplies.

5. Position yourself on a hill or overpass so that you can get a better view of the storm.

6. Respect nature.

7. Educate yourself about extreme weather events and the dangers involved.

8. Take close-up pictures or videos of victims and sell them to the highest bidder or publish them on Facebook without the victims' knowledge or permission.

9. Race to the scene; do whatever it takes to get there before anyone else.

10. Obey driving laws and rules of the road.

11. In all situations, use common sense.

12. Stop or leave your car in the middle of the road to take a picture or video.

Do's	Don'ts

Reading skills

Note-taking *Make notes for a newspaper article about storm chasers, using the following questions to develop your outline.*

1. What types of people are storm chasers?

_____

2. What do they do?

_____

_____

3. When do they chase storms?

_____

4. Where do they chase storms?

_____

5. How do they chase storms? What equipment do they need?

_____

_____

6. Why do they chase storms?

_____

_____

Web search and writing

The activities on the next two pages prompt you to share information with a study partner and to search the Web for more information about how to prepare for a natural disaster.

Natural disaster preparedness

ACTIVITY 6·1

Exchange experiences *Ask your partner the following questions, and add a question of your own.*

1. What extreme weather-related events occur where you live?

- ☐ Blizzards and snowstorms
- ☐ Drought
- ☐ Dust storms
- ☐ Forest fires
- ☐ Hailstorms

- ☐ Heat waves
- ☐ Hurricanes
- ☐ Thunderstorms
- ☐ Tornadoes
- ☐ Tsunamis

☐ _____

☐ _____

2. Do you know what to do in the event of a disaster such as a tornado, hurricane, tsunami, or earthquake? What steps would you take?

_____

_____

3. Your question _____

Discussion *Share your answers with another partner or with the whole group.*

ACTIVITY 6·2

Search the Web *Find information about how to prepare for a natural disaster, and record the following details.*

Agency or organization _____

URL   www._____

Emergency measures _____

_____

_____

_____

Agency or organization _____

URL www._____

Emergency measures _____

_____

_____

_____

Agency or organization _____

URL www._____

Emergency measures _____

_____

_____

_____

ACTIVITY
6·3

Writing *For a bulletin board at your school, create a poster outlining the steps people should take in the event of a natural disaster.*

Pixar Studios
Movie magic

Pre-reading

How often do you go to the movies? _____

What kinds of movies do you like?

☐ Action
☐ Animation
☐ Classic
☐ Comedy
☐ Documentary

☐ Drama
☐ Horror
☐ Romance
☐ Science fiction
☐ Thriller

☐ _____
☐ _____

Reading text

1   It would be impossible to imagine the movies without the magic of animation. Beginning in 1937 with Walt Disney's *Snow White and the Seven Dwarfs,* the makers of animated feature films have created some of motion pictures' most enduring characters and enchanting stories. *Pinocchio, Cinderella, Beauty and the Beast, Bambi,* and *The Lion King,* to name but a few Disney classics, continue to win the hearts of children and adults alike, but the **painstaking** process of cel animation[1] that went into their making has become a thing of the past. Computer technology, with Pixar Studios at the forefront, has **revolutionized** animated filmmaking.

Company history

2   The idea of using computer graphics to create an animated film originated in the 1970s, when the president of the New York Institute of Technology asked computer scientist Ed Catmull to make an animated film based on the song "Tubby the Tuba."[2] Instead of producing a movie, Catmull's team came up with **innovative** video artwork. In 1979, George Lucas, the creator/producer/director of *Star Wars,*

---

[1] Traditional animation, also known as cel animation, required artists to draw numerous two-dimensional frames by hand. Each frame varied slightly from the previous one, so that when shown in sequence the subject of the drawings would move. The drawings were then transferred onto acetate sheets, or cels, colored in, and photographed against a background.

[2] "Tubby the Tuba" was a musical story about a tuba that discovered it could play a melody. Written one week after the 1941 attack on Pearl Harbor, the story became an iconic symbol for Americans and achieved landmark status in audio history.

made the team part of Lucasfilm Ltd., based in California. Known as the Graphics Group, Catmull and his creative crew used the Pixar Image Computer to design graphics programs and to **generate** images and special effects with just about any subject, from animals to cars to buildings. In 1984, Lucas recruited John Lasseter, a two-time winner of Student Film Awards while at the California Institute of the Arts, from Disney Studios. That same year, Lasseter produced *André and Wally B.*, his first 3-D short. Under Lasseter's creative direction, the group would go on to **pioneer** special effects and change the face of films forever.

3   As is often the case with historical forerunners, Pixar Studios' road to success was a rocky one. Despite the graphic division's creative success, Lucas sold it in 1986 to Steve Jobs, the cofounder and ex-CEO (at the time) of Apple Computers, for $10 million. The following year, Pixar Studios won first prize in Computer-Generated Imagery at the San Francisco International Film Festival for *Luxo Jr.*, as well as its first Academy Award **nomination** for Best Animated Short. To make money for the company, Lasseter turned to animated commercials, an undertaking that would **garner** prizes and set milestones in the field of advertising. In the meantime, Pixar Studios continued to receive international nominations and prizes for its short films. Its greatest invention was RenderMan®, an innovative graphics program that could add color and textures to 3-D images with photographic quality. *Tin Toy*, the first film to use this technology, won an Academy Award for Animated Short Film in 1988.

4   Under Jobs's leadership, Pixar Studios formed a partnership in 1989 with Colossal Pictures, which gave Pixar's RenderMan technology a major boost. By 1990, well-known companies were using RenderMan to produce their graphics. Together with Colossal Pictures, Pixar made a commercial for Life Savers candy that became an outstanding success. Pixar was still not making a profit, however. In May 1991, Pixar teamed up with Walt Disney Pictures to produce three animated films. The result of this **collaboration** was *Toy Story*, the first feature-length computer-animated film and the beginning of a major **turnaround**.

5   Released on November 22, 1995, *Toy Story* made animation history. *Toy Story* and its two **sequels** recount the adventures and misadventures of a group of toys under the leadership of lovable favorites Woody and Buzz Lightyear, who come to life when their owner Andy Davis is not present. Hugely popular with audiences around the world, *Toy Story* was the top-grossing film of 1995, bringing in $362 million globally at box offices. For his leadership role in the production of *Toy Story*, the Academy of Motion Pictures and Sciences awarded John Lasseter a Special **Achievement** Award.

6   Following on *Toy Story*'s success, Pixar agreed in 1997 to produce another five feature films for Disney: *A Bug's Life*; *Monsters, Inc.*; *Finding Nemo*; *The Incredibles*; and *Cars*. The agreement was subsequently expanded to include *Toy Story 2* in 1999 and *Ratatouille* in 2006. Together with Disney Studios Motion Pictures, Pixar Animation Studios went on to produce 10 feature films, which together have grossed in excess of $6 billion and earned the company 35 Academy Award nominations, nine Oscars, and six Golden Globes, plus several international awards. In 2004, *Finding Nemo* took home the Oscar for Best Animated Film.

How a film is made

7   A Pixar movie begins with an idea for a story. If the employee with the idea can sell it to the development team, the next step is to write different versions of the story in summary form, called treatments. Artists then draw storyboards that resemble comic book sequences and develop the storyline and its characters. If the story meets with the director's **approval**, the script is written and employees record the first voices. The dialogue is perfected and professional actors are hired to read the parts. The best versions are made into a videotape, or reel, which goes to editing for clean-up. After that, the art department creates the visuals: characters, set, props, lighting—everything that appears on the movie screen.

8   Models of the characters are then sculpted by hand, or scanned or modeled in 3-D into the computer, and given "avars," or hinges, which the animator uses to make the figures move. Next, the scenes are laid out with the characters in place on 3-D sets. Several shots of each scene are taken so that editors can choose the scene that best tells the story. The final cut goes to animation, where animators use software to **manipulate** the characters' movements and facial expressions. Using a technique called "shading," animators adjust colors and textures to make the characters come to life. Lighting is then added to create the emotional tone of a scene. Finally, all the files are fed into a huge computer system, where they undergo "rendering," a complex and time-consuming process that combines all the data into single movie frames. When the musical score and special sound effects are added, the photoscience department records the final product for digital projection, and the film is ready for viewing.

The future

9   In 2006, Pixar Studios **merged** with the Walt Disney Company. In the span of nine years, Pixar has broken new ground in the field of computer graphics. The vision, passion, and commitment to excellence that drive the company have made Pixar an **unprecedented** financial and artistic success. As Pixar Studios continues under Catmull's and Lasseter's leadership to promote creative talent and bring memorable stories to the screen, it will keep its place in the hearts of moviegoers for generations to come.

Pixar Studios feature films

Movie	Year	Main characters	Storyline
Toy Story	1995	Woody, Buzz Lightyear	Woody feels abandoned after Andy gets a new toy.
A Bug's Life	1998	Flik	Flik must use his inventiveness to save the ant colony from invading grasshoppers.
Toy Story 2	1999	Woody, Buzz Lightyear, and the toy gang	Woody's toy friends must save him from the hands of a nasty toy collector.
Monsters, Inc.	2001	James P. Sullivan, Mike	Monsters Sully and Mike must return a human girl to her home from Monstropolis.
Finding Nemo	2003	Marlin, Dory, Nemo	Marlin and his friend go on a dangerous mission to rescue Marlin's son, Nemo, who is taken from the coral reef by a diver.
The Incredibles	2004	The Incredible family	A family of superheroes living a boring life in suburbia are called into action to save the day.
Cars	2006	Lightning McQueen	Racecar McQueen takes a detour on Route 66 and ends up in a small community.
Ratatouille	2007	Remy	Aspiring gourmet chef Remy gets a chance to prove his culinary talents in a Paris restaurant.

Movie	Year	Main characters	Storyline
WALL·E	2008	WALL·E, EVE	While on an adventure across the galaxy, robot WALL·E discovers how to save the earth's future.
Up	2009	Carl Fredrikson, Russell	An elderly balloon salesman and a young stowaway fly away to South America on an adventure.
Toy Story 3	2010	Woody, Buzz Lightyear, and the toy gang	When Andy goes to college, the toys must stick together after they end up in the hands of grabby children.
Cars 2	2011	Lightning McQueen, Mater	McQueen and Mater travel overseas to race in the World Grand Prix only to find themselves caught up in an international intrigue.
Brave	2012	Merida, King Fergus, Queen Elinor	Merida defies the customs of her kingdom and is faced with the task of breaking a fateful curse.

Vocabulary

EXERCISE 7·1

Organizing vocabulary *List the words and phrases from the reading text that relate to the following categories. An example has been provided for each category.*

1. A synonym for *movie* (3) *feature film,* _____

2. People who work on a movie (7) *creator,* _____

_____

3. Components of a scene (6) *special effects,* _____

_____

Understanding vocabulary *Indicate the part of speech (n., v., or adj.) of each word in the following list. Then, using a dictionary, indicate the word's definition.*

Word and part of speech   Definition

1. achievement _____   _____

2. nomination _____   _____

3. collaboration _____   _____

4. turnaround _____   _____

5. sequel _____   _____

6. approval _____   _____

7. revolutionize _____   _____

8. generate _____   _____

9. pioneer _____   _____

10. manipulate _____   _____

11. merge _____   _____

12. garner _____   _____

13. innovative _____   _____

14. painstaking _____   _____

15. unprecedented _____   _____

Using vocabulary *Complete each of the following sentences with the appropriate word(s) from the list in Exercise 7-2. Be sure to use the correct form of each verb and to pluralize nouns, if necessary.*

1. In order to go on the class ski trip, all students will have to get written

   _____ from their parents.

2. The government's decision to increase the penalty for those who drive over the speed

   limit has _____ a lot of public discussion.

3. The two companies decided to _____ in order to combine their experience and resources.

4. The television series *Mad Men* _____ several Emmy

   _____ and awards.

5. Apple is known for its _____ iPhone and iPad.

6. When the old coach resigned and the new coach took over, the basketball team experienced a complete _____ in its performance.

7. Pixar Studios has made two _____ to *Toy Story* and one to *Cars*.

8. You can make a puppet dance by _____ the strings attached to its body and limbs.

9. Making an animated movie requires the _____ of all members of the production team, including script writers, editors, and graphic artists.

10. Cell phones have _____ communication.

11. The number of times that American actress Meryl Streep has been nominated for an Academy Award is _____.

12. NASA's first manned landing on the moon on July 20, 1969, was a remarkable

    _____.

13. Orville and Wilbur Wright _____ manned flight and invented the first airplane.

14. Efforts to restore the Frauenkirche in Dresden to its original condition and beauty were

    _____, time-consuming, and very costly.

Reading comprehension

EXERCISE
7·4

Reading for main ideas *For each of the following sentences, choose the correct answer to fill in the blank.*

1. Pixar Studios was the first film production company to make animated films using

    _____.
    a. cel animation
    b. computer graphics
    c. models

2. From the beginning, Pixar Studios has been _____.
    a. financially profitable
    b. independently managed
    c. artistically successful

3. Pixar Studios' most revolutionary technological development was _____.
    a. a computer graphics program called RenderMan®
    b. avar hinges to move and manipulate characters
    c. the Pixar Image Computer

4. Pixar Studios was able to generate revenue by _____.
   a. selling the Pixar Image Computer
   b. creating and producing animated commercials
   c. winning awards

5. The film _____ made animation history.
   a. *Toy Story*
   b. *Finding Nemo*
   c. *The Incredibles*

6. Pixar Studios' animated films have won _____.
   a. Academy Awards
   b. Golden Globe Awards
   c. Academy Awards, Golden Globe Awards, and international awards

7. Under the leadership of Ed Catmull and John Lasseter, Pixar Studios has achieved artistic and financial success in _____.
   a. less than a decade
   b. two decades
   c. three decades

EXERCISE
7·5

Reading for details *Number the 14 steps below to show the sequence of making an animated film.*

_____ Professional actors read and record the characters' parts, and the videotape is edited.

_____ The musical score and special effects are added.

_____ Artists draw storyboards.

_____ Colors, textures, and lighting are adjusted to make the characters come to life and to set the tone of the film.

_____ The film is made for projection.

_____ The final script is written.

_____ An employee comes up with an idea for a movie and sells it to the development team.

_____ Scenes with the characters are planned out and recorded.

_____ The director approves the story.

_____ Models of the characters are made.

_____ Different treatments of the story are written.

_____ All the files are fed into a computer for "rendering."

_____ The art department creates all the visuals for the characters, set, props, and lighting.

_____ The scenes are edited into a final cut, which goes to the animators for animation.

Reading for facts and figures *Rewrite the following sentences, correcting the errors. Some statements may have more than one error.*

1. Pixar Studios was founded in the 1930s.

   _____

2. In 1984, Lucas recruited Ed Catmull, a two-time winner of Academy Awards, from Disney Studios.

   _____

   _____

3. Despite the graphic division's creative success, Lucas sold the group to Bill Gates for $1 million.

   _____

   _____

4. *Toy Story*, the first film to use this technology, won an Academy Award for Best Animated Feature Film in 1988.

   _____

   _____

5. In May 1991, Pixar teamed up with Colossal Pictures to produce five animated films.

   _____

6. Hugely popular with audiences around the world, *Toy Story* became the top-grossing film of 1998, bringing in $262 million globally at box offices.

   _____

   _____

7. Together with Disney Studios Motion Pictures, Pixar Animation Studios went on to produce seven feature films.

   _____

   _____

8. Pixar's films have earned the company three Academy Award nominations, two Oscars, and four Golden Globes, plus a few international awards.

   _____

   _____

9. In 2004, *The Incredibles* took home a Golden Globe for Best Animated Film.

   _____

10. In 2006, Pixar merged with Lucasfilm Ltd.

   _____

Reading for meaning *Indicate whether each of the following statements from the reading text is an example of Pixar Studios' success or not.*

1. "Computer technology, with Pixar Studios at the forefront, has revolutionized animated filmmaking."
   ☐ Successful
   ☐ Unsuccessful

2. "As is often the case with historical forerunners, Pixar Studios' road to success was a rocky one."
   ☐ Successful
   ☐ Unsuccessful

3. "Instead of producing a movie, Catmull's team came up with innovative video artwork."
   ☐ Successful
   ☐ Unsuccessful

4. "Under Lasseter's creative direction, the group would go to pioneer special effects and change the face of films forever."
   ☐ Successful
   ☐ Unsuccessful

5. "To make money for the company, Lasseter turned to animated commercials, an undertaking that would garner prizes and set milestones in the field of advertising."
   ☐ Successful
   ☐ Unsuccessful

Reading skills

Summary *Summarize the milestones in Pixar Studios' road to success.*

1979 _____
_____

1984 _____
_____

1986 _____
_____

1987 _____
_____

1988 _____
_____

1995 _____
_____

1997 _____
_____

2004 _____
_____

2006 _____
_____

Web search and writing

The activities on the next two pages prompt you to share information with a study partner and to search the Web for more information about animated films.

Famous animated movies

ACTIVITY 7·1

Exchange experiences *Ask your partner the following questions, and add a question of your own.*

1. What is your favorite animated film? _____

   How many times have you seen it? _____

   What do you like best about your favorite animated film?

   ☐ The artwork   ☐ The special effects
   ☐ The characters   ☐ The story
   ☐ The music   ☐ The voices

   ☐ _____   ☐ _____

2. What film companies besides Pixar Studios are famous for their animated films?

   _____

3. Your question _____

Discussion *Share your answers with another partner or with the whole group.*

ACTIVITY 7·2

Search the Web *Find information about famous animated films, and record the following details.*

Name of film   _____

URL   www._____

Main characters _____
and storyline   _____

                   _____

                   _____

Name of film   _____

URL   www._____

Main characters   _____
and storyline   _____

_____

_____

Name of film   _____

URL   www._____

Main characters   _____
and storyline   _____

_____

_____

_____

ACTIVITY
7·3

Writing *Imagine that you make animated films. Create a story outline for an animated film. What is the name of your film? Who are the main characters? What happens in your film?*

Karaoke
Everyone can be a star

Pre-reading

What kinds of music do you like?

☐ Blues
☐ Classical
☐ Country and western
☐ Easy listening
☐ Folk and traditional

☐ Heavy metal
☐ Jazz
☐ Pop
☐ Rap/hip-hop
☐ Rock

☐ _____

☐ _____

Do you like to sing? Are you a good singer? _____

Reading text

1   Have you ever wanted to sing like Michael Jackson, Madonna, Elvis Presley, Taylor Swift, or Beyoncé? If you like to get up in public and sing your favorite ABBA or Beatles song, then karaoke is for you. You can sing karaoke in a bar or club that hosts popular "Karaoke Nights," or if you'd prefer not to perform in front of strangers, you can rent a special karaoke room, called a "karaoke box," with a group of friends. Of course, you can get your own karaoke machine and sing to your heart's content at home, but half the fun is letting your hair down, belting it out, and possibly making a fool of yourself, just like millions of people have been doing all over the world since karaoke became a **craze**.

2   *Karaoke,* which means "empty orchestra" in Japanese, got its start in Kobe, Japan, in the late 1960s. Daisuke Inoue, a former nightclub musician and percussionist, was asked to **accompany** a business man on a trip so that the man could sing to his friends. Rather than carting along his instruments, Inoue recorded the CEO's favorite song on 8-track tape and gave it to him to use as a backup sound track. Inoue then came up with the idea to build a music machine containing an 8-track tape player, a small amplifier, and a box in which to **insert** 100-yen coins. He leased his machines out, but he **neglected** to patent his invention. Although Daisuke Inoue is **credited** with inventing karaoke, it was Filipino inventor Roberto del Rosario who patented his sing-along system, Minus-One, which became the forerunner of the modern karaoke machine.[1]

---

[1] *Karaoke* may also refer to the backup tapes, or "canned" music, that professional singers in Japan use when they are performing without a band.

3   Karaoke quickly took off in Japanese bars and clubs, where businessmen, in particular, could exercise their vocal cords after a few drinks. From an entertaining pastime, karaoke has developed into big business: annual revenues for karaoke clubs in Japan are estimated at $4.5 billion. Karaoke venues have evolved from a simple shipping container or railway boxcar to rent-by-the-hour karaoke rooms to multistory complexes. There are family karaoke restaurants and exclusive private clubs, mega-karaoke **facilities** that resemble **kitschy** theme parks, and karaoke chain stores that specialize in state-of-the-art equipment. Karaoke clubs are open 24/7, and an evening of karaoke can include food and drinks in the price.

4   In the 1990s, karaoke spread throughout Asia. Whether in Manila or Seoul, Taipei or Bangkok, Hong Kong or Singapore, Hanoi or Jakarta, karaoke was **catching on**. By 2009, an average of 1.9 million South Koreans were singing **renditions** of their favorite songs in 35,684 "song rooms." In China, thousands of popular KTVs—karaoke television bars—sprang up and included private gaming rooms. The longest nonstop karaoke rally (lasting 456 hours, two minutes and five seconds) was held in China between February 20 and March 11, 2009.

5   It didn't take long for karaoke to make it to Europe, North America, and Australia, where bar patrons can sing for free, usually on a small stage. Karaoke Nights attract faithful crowds of regulars, and special theme nights or contests are held, with prizes awarded to the best performer. Some countries, such as Finland, take karaoke very seriously. On May 26, 2006, Finland made it into the *Guinness World Records* when 80,000 people sang "Hard Rock Hallelujah" in celebration of the rock band Lordi's **triumph** at the Eurovision Song Contest. Since 2003, a group of Finnish producers has been organizing the Karaoke World Championship. The now **prestigious** international event has been hosted in Finland, Thailand, Russia, and Ireland, with talented singers from more than 30 countries **vying** for the top three male and female titles.

6   Karaoke has not only come a long distance, but it has come a long way from Inoue's original box. Soon, 8-tracks were replaced by cassette tapes, which in turn were replaced by CDs, VCDs, laser disc, and DVDs. Singers choose from a wide range of pop, country and western, Broadway, and evergreen songs, and they can also change the key to suit their vocal range. The **lyrics** appear on a screen complete with a video theme background, which gives the performance an MTV feel, and a bouncing ball so the singer can keep up with the music. Karaoke is also available for mobile phones and computers, and existing software lets singers share their passion over the Internet.

7   Thanks to karaoke, more people are getting up the nerve to sing, and as research has shown, singing has definite physiological and psychological benefits. Like exercise, singing is an aerobic activity that increases our oxygen intake and boosts the cardiovascular system. When we sing, we breathe more deeply, and this helps us relax and reduces stress. Research shows that singing releases endorphins—"feel good" chemicals—into the bloodstream, elevating our mood. Provided we can overcome our shyness, getting up and singing can **bolster** confidence. Since most songs are about love, singing allows us to express our feelings and to reach out to others, which is why we feel such a personal connection to our favorite singers. In a nutshell, singing is good for our bodies, our hearts, and our souls.

8   So let's say you're not tone deaf and you've got a pretty good voice. How can you sing like a pro? Here are some tips that will put you in the limelight.

- **Song** Choose a song you like, but make sure it suits your voice and vocal range. You may really love Simon and Garfunkel's "Bridge over Troubled Water," but if you can't hit the high notes at the end, you're headed for **embarrassment**.
- **Breathing** Professionals breathe with their diaphragm, which is below your rib cage. This allows your lungs to expand, so that you don't run out of breath in the middle of a word or before you finish a line. This takes practice, but if you can master this breathing technique, your voice will be stronger and you'll have greater control.
- **Voice** Keep your larynx (voice box) low and let your voice come from the bottom of your throat. Otherwise, you may strain your vocal cords and sound screechy. If you place your hand

at the base of your throat, below your larynx, and hum, you can feel the vibration of your vocal cords.

♦ **Posture** Even if you're nervous, relax and loosen up. Move to the rhythm if it makes you more comfortable, and don't worry about what others may think. If you're having fun, so will everyone else.

♦ **Smile and sing from your heart.**

9   You might not make it to the finals of *American Idol* or be offered a recording contract, but you'll be amazed at how much fun you can have. And isn't that what karaoke is all about?

Top 12 karaoke songs[2]

Song	Artist
1. "Waterloo"	ABBA
2. "Bohemian Rhapsody"	Queen
3. "My Way"	Frank Sinatra
4. "I Will Survive"	Gloria Gaynor
5. "Dancing Queen"	ABBA
6. "Angels"	Robbie Williams
7. "Like a Virgin"	Madonna
8. "It's Raining Men"	The Weather Girls
9. "Summer Nights"	Olivia Newton-John and John Travolta
10. "I Should Be So Lucky"	Kylie Minogue
11. "Don't Go Breaking My Heart"	Elton John and Kiki Dee
12. "Sweet Caroline"	Neil Diamond

---

[2]From http://www.telegraph.co.uk.

Vocabulary

EXERCISE

8·1

Organizing vocabulary *List the words and phrases from the reading text that relate to the following headings. Add the part of speech (n., v., or adj.) for each word or phrase. An example has been provided for each heading.*

Musical performers	**Singing**	**Music recording**
orchestra (n.)	*song (n.)*	*8-track (adj.)*

EXERCISE
8·2

Understanding vocabulary *Match each word or phrase in column 1 with its definition in column 2. Then, indicate each item's part of speech (n., v., or adj.).*

_____ 1. craze _____
_____ 2. accompany _____
_____ 3. insert _____
_____ 4. neglect _____
_____ 5. credit _____
_____ 6. embarrassment _____
_____ 7. facility _____
_____ 8. kitschy _____
_____ 9. catch on _____
_____ 10. rendition _____
_____ 11. triumph _____
_____ 12. prestigious _____
_____ 13. bolster _____
_____ 14. lyrics _____
_____ 15. vie _____

a. a way that something is presented or interpreted
b. believe that someone has done something
c. compete eagerly to achieve something
d. a building or service provided for a specific purpose
e. widespread but short-lived enthusiasm for something
f. a great achievement or success
g. place or fit something into something else
h. having or bringing respect or admiration
i. support or strengthen
j. go somewhere with someone
k. showing bad taste or sentimentalism
l. the words of a song or short poem
m. fail to do something
n. become popular
o. a feeling of self-consciousness, shame, or awkwardness

Understanding vocabulary *Match each of the following definitions with the corresponding underlined idiom in the numbered items below.*

a. In short / In the fewest words possible
b. When someone finds the courage to do something
c. When something becomes popular very fast
d. When you do something that makes you really happy
e. When something makes you the center of attention
f. When you enjoy yourself without feeling self-conscious

_____ 1. "Of course, you can get your own karaoke machine and sing <u>to your heart's content</u> at home."

_____ 2. "Half the fun is <u>letting your hair down</u>."

_____ 3. "<u>In a nutshell</u>, singing is good for our bodies, our hearts, and our souls."

_____ 4. "Here are some tips that will put you <u>in the limelight</u>."

_____ 5. "Thanks to karaoke, more people <u>are getting up the nerve</u> to sing."

_____ 6. "Karaoke quickly <u>took off</u> in Japanese bars and clubs."

Using vocabulary *Create a sentence from each of the phrases or clauses below. The boldface word is from the reading text.*

EXAMPLE   a popular dance **craze**

The Macarena was a popular dance craze in the mid-1990s.

1. a recent fashion **craze**

_____

2. **accompany** a friend on a trip

_____

3. **insert** a bank card into an ATM

_____

4. **neglect** to study for an exam

_____

5. **credit** someone with an invention

_____

6. a terrible **embarrassment** by forgetting something

_____

7. a large shopping **facility**

_____

8. a **kitschy** souvenir

_____

9. a slang phrase or expression that **is catching on**

_____

10. a **rendition** of a well-known song

_____

11. a significant **triumph** in a sports event

_____

12. a **prestigious** university or college

_____

13. something that **bolsters** your mood when you're feeling sad

_____

14. a song with **lyrics** that are easy to understand

_____

15. **vie** for the attention of someone important or attractive

_____

Reading comprehension

EXERCISE
8·5

Reading for main ideas _Indicate which of the following statements are true (T) and which are false (F)._

1. _____ Karaoke originated in the Philippines and spread to other countries in Asia and the rest of the world.

2. _____ Karaoke singers can choose from a wide variety of music and change the key of the music to fit their vocal range.

3. _____ People sing karaoke mostly in their homes or at private gatherings.

4. _____ Karaoke has positive health benefits.

5. _____ Karaoke has become a profitable business and has developed into an entertainment industry all its own.

6. _____ Karaoke is only for professional singers.

Reading for details *Answer the following questions, using information from the reading text. Try not to copy directly from the text.*

1. What does the word *karaoke* mean?

   _____

2. What is a "karaoke box"?

   _____

3. Where do people usually sing karaoke?

   _____

4. What types of music can people choose from?

   _____

5. How do people know the lyrics to sing?

   _____

6. What are the health benefits of singing?

   _____

7. What should singers keep in mind when they choose a song?

   _____

8. How should singers breathe when they sing?

   _____

9. Why should singers try to keep their voice low when they sing?

   _____

10. What's the most important thing to remember when you sing karaoke?

   _____

Reading for facts and figures *Choose the boldface word or phrase that correctly completes each of the following statements.*

1. **Daisuke Inoue | Roberto del Rosario** invented karaoke.
2. **Daisuke Inoue | Roberto del Rosario** patented the first karaoke machine.
3. Karaoke started out in the city of **Tokyo | Kobe**.
4. From Japan, karaoke soon spread to **Asia | North America** in the 1990s.
5. The first karaoke music was recorded on **8-track tapes | compact discs**.

Karaoke: Everyone can be a star   **91**

6. The longest nonstop karaoke event took place in **Finland** | **China**.

7. The largest group of karaoke singers in a single performance numbered **8,000** | **80,000**.

8. The Karaoke World Championship was first organized in 2003 by a group of
   Finnish | **American** producers.

9. The most popular karaoke song was originally recorded by **ABBA** | **the Beatles**.

10. Karaoke clubs in Japan earn about **4.5** | **5.4** billion dollars a year.

EXERCISE
8·8

Reading for meaning *Indicate which of the following are or are not reasons
to sing karaoke.*

	Yes	No
1. Karaoke sometimes involves singing in front of strangers.	☐	☐
2. There is a wide variety of venues in which people can sing karaoke.	☐	☐
3. Singing releases endorphins into the bloodstream.	☐	☐
4. You can make a fool of yourself.	☐	☐
5. In North America, Europe, and Australia, people can sing for free.	☐	☐
6. You can sing at karaoke theme nights and win prizes in competitions.	☐	☐
7. Karaoke clubs are open 24/7.	☐	☐

Reading skills

Outline *Use the outline below to indicate the most important details from the reading text. Then, use your outline to write a summary of 350 to 400 words. Try not to copy directly from the text.*

The history of karaoke

    Meaning of *karaoke* _____

    Inventor _____

    The first karaoke machine _____

The popularity of karaoke

    Karaoke venues _____

    Karaoke businesses _____

    The spread of karaoke _____

    Karaoke events and contests _____

The mechanics of karaoke

    Technology _____

    Songs _____

    Performance _____

The benefits of singing karaoke

    Physiological benefits _____

    Psychological benefits _____

Singing tips

    Choosing a song _____

    Breathing _____

    Voice _____

    Posture _____

Web search and writing

The activities on the next two pages prompt you to share information with a study partner and to search the Web for more information about your favorite singers.

Famous singers

ACTIVITY
8·1

Exchange experiences *Ask your partner the following questions, and add a question of your own.*

1. Which famous singers are you familiar with?

☐ Beyoncé   ☐ Michael Jackson
☐ Justin Bieber   ☐ Avril Lavigne
☐ Mariah Carey   ☐ Madonna
☐ Lady Gaga   ☐ Elvis Presley
☐ Enrico Iglesias   ☐ Britney Spears

☐ _____   ☐ _____

2. Who are your favorite singers? Which songs of theirs do you like?

_____

_____

_____

3. Your question _____

Discussion *Share your answers with another partner or with the whole group.*

ACTIVITY
8·2

Search the Web *Find information about famous singers, their music, and their careers, and record the following details.*

Name of singer   _____

URL   www._____

Most famous songs   _____

                        _____

                        _____

Biographical information _____

                        _____

                        _____

Name of singer   _____

URL   www._____

Most famous songs   _____

_____

_____

Biographical information   _____

_____

_____

Name of singer   _____

URL   www._____

Most famous songs   _____

_____

_____

Biographical information   _____

_____

_____

ACTIVITY

8·3

Writing *Write a list of questions that you would like to ask your favorite singer if you had the chance to interview him or her.*

The flying doctors of Australia
Reaching "the furthest corner"

Pre-reading

Which of the following medical services does your community offer?

- ☐ Ambulance
- ☐ Dentists
- ☐ Family doctors/general practitioners
- ☐ Hospitals
- ☐ Medical laboratories

- ☐ Mental health services
- ☐ Pharmacists
- ☐ Physiotherapy
- ☐ Specialists
- ☐ Walk-in clinics

What is the quality of health care services in your community?

Reading text

1   In developed countries, medical care is **taken for granted**. Of course, you need to make an appointment first, and you may have to wait an hour or longer before your doctor can see you, but when you need medical treatment, a doctor is as close to your home as the nearest store. There may even be doctors in your neighborhood who make house calls, and in the case of an emergency, an ambulance will rush you to the hospital. But what if you live in an isolated area, and to reach the nearest medical facility, you must travel a long distance if you can travel at all? And what if you are poor and have no medical insurance? If you live in Australia's outback, the doctor will come to you free of charge, and as a member of the Royal Flying Doctor Service, the doctor will come in an airplane.

2   At the turn of the twentieth century, only two doctors served Australia's outback, a **remote** area of nearly two million square kilometers stretching from the continent's southernmost tip to Darwin in the north. A firsthand **witness** to the struggles of settlers and laborers in a vast, scorched country, Reverend John Flynn, a Presbyterian minister, began setting up nursing hostels and bush hospitals. In 1912, he founded the Australian Inland Mission to tend to the spiritual, social, and medical needs of the rural population. In his magazine, *The Inlander*, Reverend Flynn informed his readers about the difficulties faced by settlers and aboriginals living in the bush, and he called for **urgent** action. His experiences led him to seek a way to provide a "mantle of safety" that would ensure more reliable and immediate medical services.

3   In 1917, Reverend Flynn received a letter from a young airman and medical student from Victoria, who suggested flying medical help into remote areas. Unfortunately, Lieutenant Clifford Peel was killed in combat in France, but his

96

letter inspired Reverend Flynn to raise funding for an aerial medical service. After 10 years, Flynn had gathered financing from business associations, the Presbyterian Church, and government agencies, as well as from personal supporters like businessman H. V. McKay, who bequeathed £2,000 to the mission, and Hudson Fysh, one of the founders of Queensland and Northern Territory Air Service (QANTAS). On May 17, 1928, the Australian Inland Mission Aerial Medical Service, the first of its kind in the world, flew *Victory*, a fabric-covered, single-engine de Havilland DH.50 biplane, leased at a rate of two shillings per mile, from Fysh's aviation company in Cloncurry to Julia Creek. The service's first two employees, pilot Arthur Affleck and Dr. Kenyon St Vincent Welch, were on board.

4   In its first year, the Aerial Medical Service flew 50 flights, covered 18,000 miles, and helped 225 patients in 26 locations, despite considerable risks and **obstacles**. The first de Havilland airplanes could fly a maximum distance of 600 miles at a speed of 80 miles an hour, and could carry no more than four passengers at a time. Pilots flew in open cockpits exposed to all kinds of weather, with no maps and only a compass to **navigate** by; they had to follow rivers, fences, telegraph lines, roads, wheel tracks, and landmarks to their destinations. Until fueling stations were set up, pilots had to carry fuel with them, and landing on rough **terrain** or makeshift clearings was an adventure in itself. Sometimes, sheets were laid on the ground or flares were lit to mark the landing strip. Most flights were made during the day, but in cases of extreme emergency, pilots flew night missions.

5   While flying to isolated locations presented **challenges** in the air, contact between residents and doctors was a problem on the ground. At the time, the telegraph was the only means of communication, and Flynn was well aware that the effective delivery of medical service depended on communication. Even before his project got off the ground, Flynn and George Town, an army radio technician, were **conducting** unsuccessful experiments to generate electricity to power radio transmitters. When Alfred Traeger, an engineer who started working for Flynn in 1926, invented the pedal-operated generator, isolated homesteaders could finally make contact with the outside world. As radio technology developed and took over, emergency call systems began **linking** stations, missions, and residences with doctors, hospitals, and other **vital** services.

6   In 1930, the Australian Inland Mission Aerial Medical Service changed its name to the Aerial Medical Service. By 1937, it had opened five sections in Victoria, New South Wales, South Australia, Western Australia, and the Eastern Gold Fields, with eight bases in outlying places such as Alice Springs, Kalgoorlie, and Broken Hill. Queensland was added in 1939, and Tasmania in 1960. In 1942, the service became known as the Flying Doctor Service, and in 1955, it was officially renamed the Royal Flying Doctor Service in honor of its contributions "to the effective settlement of the far distant country that we have witnessed in our time" (Prime Minister Sir Robert Menzies).

7   In keeping with its goal of providing first-class health service to everyone living, working, or traveling in the remote areas of Australia, the RFDS has continuously updated its flight and equipment capacity. In its early days, contractors supplied the RFDS with aircraft and pilots, but after the 1960s, the RFDS began to purchase its own aircraft and hire its own pilots and service crews. Now, the RFDS owns 60 King Air, PC-12, and Cessna 208B Grand Caravan airplanes, and these airborne intensive-care units operate on battery power and contain resuscitation devices, neonatal incubators, and medical oxygen and suction systems. The communication system facilitates contact between the pilot and medical staff, which typically consists of one doctor and one nurse, with a second doctor available to assist in cases of serious illness or **injury**.

8   To accomplish its mission of providing excellence in aeromedical and primary health care across Australia, the RFDS **maintains** a network of seven sections with 21 bases, 5 clinics, and 10 offices including its national office in Sydney, and it operates 24-hour emergency and transport services across Australia. Users of the service receive general medical care and health screening in addition to a broad range of specialized services, such as immunization and mental health care.

RFDS employs a staff of 977, consisting of pilots, technicians, doctors, nurses, dentists, aboriginal and Torres Strait health workers, and management and administrative staff. In addition to **treating** accident victims and sick patients on-site, doctors and nurses are available for radio consultations. As a nonprofit organization, the RFDS treats its patients and users free of charge; it relies on federal government funding and charitable donations from businesses and the general public.

9   The following figures (for the year ending June 30, 2010) demonstrate how vital the RFDS has become to the health and safety of rural Australians.

Service	Daily average	Yearly total
Patient contacts	758	276,489
Patient transports	106	38,852
Distance flown (kilometers)	70,116	25,592,455
Landings	203	74,214

SOURCE RFDS annual report, 2010–2011.

10   In 2009, the RFDS modernized its logo and adopted a new slogan: *The furthest corner. The finest care.* More than 80 years after its establishment, the RFDS remains **committed** to keeping Reverend John Flynn's dream alive and well.

Vocabulary

EXERCISE
9·1

Organizing vocabulary *List the words and phrases from the reading text that relate to the following headings. Add the part of speech (n., v., or adj.) for each word or phrase. An example has been provided for each heading.*

Flying	Medical services	Medical equipment
airborne (adj.)	ambulance (n.)	intensive care unit (n.)

Understanding vocabulary *Match each word or phrase in column 1 with its definition in column 2. Then, indicate each item's part of speech (n., v., adj., or phr. for phrase).*

_____ 1. take for granted _____
_____ 2. remote _____
_____ 3. witness _____
_____ 4. injury _____
_____ 5. obstacle _____
_____ 6. navigate _____
_____ 7. terrain _____
_____ 8. challenge _____
_____ 9. conduct _____
_____ 10. vital _____
_____ 11. link _____
_____ 12. maintain _____
_____ 13. committed _____
_____ 14. treat _____
_____ 15. urgent _____

a. essential, crucial
b. wound, physical damage
c. give medical care to, nurse
d. not appreciate, assume
e. problem, test
f. devoted, dedicated
g. isolated, inaccessible
h. join, connect
i. steer, guide
j. critical, pressing
k. run, carry out
l. observer, spectator
m. land, ground
n. barrier, hindrance
o. look after, keep going

Using vocabulary *Complete each of the following sentences with the appropriate word from the list in Exercise 9-2. Be sure to use the correct form of each verb and to pluralize nouns, if necessary.*

1. The doctor _____ the patient's infection with antibiotics.

2. If you want to drive over rough _____, you will need a vehicle with four-wheel drive.

3. People who live in _____ communities depend on airplanes to receive food and medical supplies.

4. Our organization is _____ to helping poor families in any way it can.

5. The drug company _____ a lot of research before it developed the new medicine.

6. When the man had a heart attack, his wife made an _____ call to 911.

7. Through television news reports, we are daily _____ to human suffering and tragedy.

8. Good health is something we shouldn't _____.

9. In order to pass this course, you have to _____ an average of 65 percent or better.

10. Fear is a major psychological _____ that everyone must learn to overcome.

11. Clean water is _____ to human survival.

12. Some people like to climb mountains, because they need a physical and mental _____.

13. When you are driving in a foreign country, it helps to have a passenger in the front seat who knows how to read a map and _____.

14. When the accident victims were taken to the hospital, the emergency doctors treated their _____.

15. Social networks such as Facebook and Twitter _____ friends and family all over the world.

Reading comprehension

EXERCISE 9·4

Reading for main ideas *Match each of the following statements with the corresponding paragraph of the reading text.*

_____ Paragraph 1

_____ Paragraph 2

_____ Paragraph 3

_____ Paragraph 4

_____ Paragraph 5

_____ Paragraph 6

_____ Paragraph 7

_____ Paragraph 8

_____ Paragraph 9

a. The service expands throughout Australia and becomes the official Royal Flying Doctor Service of Australia in 1955.

b. The Australian Inland Mission Aerial Medical Service overcomes risks and obstacles in its first year to serve patients in 26 locations.

c. Reverend Flynn raises money to establish the Australian Inland Mission Aerial Medical Service on May 17, 1928.

d. The RFDS has become an increasingly vital service to rural Australians.

e. The pedal-operated generator and developments in radio technology make communication between settlers and medical services possible.

f. The Royal Flying Doctor Service flies doctors to isolated people in Australia's outback.

g. The RFDS purchases its own airplanes and updates its equipment and services in order to provide first-class service.

h. Reverend John Flynn identifies the need for more immediate medical care for rural settlers and aborigines.

i. Today, the RFDS operates as a nonprofit organization with a broad-based network of medical centers and health care professionals, and offers comprehensive medical services free of charge throughout Australia.

Reading for details *Complete the following sentences with details from the reading text.*

1. Reverend John Flynn was a _____ minister who founded the

   _____ to help the rural population living in Australia's

   _____.

2. He dreamed of setting up a "mantle of safety" to provide _____ to settlers, laborers, and aborigines.

3. Reverend Flynn was inspired to found an aerial medical service by a suggestion from

   _____.

4. It took Flynn _____ years to raise money to start the Australian Inland Mission Aerial Medical Service.

5. Flynn received financial support from the following.

   _____

   _____

   _____

   _____

6. In its first year, the Australian Inland Mission Aerial Medical Service faced the following risks and obstacles.

   _____

   _____

   _____

   _____

   _____

   _____

7. Alfred Traeger's invention of the _____ made it possible for homesteaders to communicate with the outside world.

Reading for facts and figures *Complete the following chart with facts and figures contrasting the RFDS's beginnings with its current status.*

	Australian Inland Mission Aerial Medical Service (first year)	Royal Flying Doctor Service of Australia (current)
1. Number of medical professionals on board	_____	_____
2. Number of flights in one year	_____	_____
3. Number of patients helped	_____	_____
4. Number of destinations/landings	_____	_____
5. Distance flown	_____	_____
6. Number of aircraft	_____	_____
7. Type of aircraft used	_____	_____
8. Source of aircraft	_____	_____
9. Number of bases (by 1937)	_____	_____
10. Number of employees	_____	_____
11. Cost of medical service	_____	_____

Reading for meaning *"Do not pray for tasks equal to your powers; pray for powers equal to your tasks."—Reverend John Flynn*

1. What did Reverend Flynn mean by this statement?

_____

_____

2. Reverence Flynn's experiences in the outback led him to seek a way to provide a "mantle of safety" for the residents. What did he mean by this expression?

_____

_____

3. Has the Royal Flying Doctors Service been able to provide Reverend Flynn's "mantle of safety"? Provide supporting evidence from the reading text.

_____

_____

Reading skills

EXERCISE 9·8

Summary *Write a one-page brochure about the Royal Flying Doctor Service of Australia, including details under the following headings.*

The Royal Flying Doctor Service of Australia

Our motto

_____

Our mission

_____

Our headquarters

_____

Our founder

_____

Our history

    1928 _____

    1930 _____

    1942 _____

    1955 _____

Our achievements

_____

_____

_____

_____

Our staff

_____

Our services

_____

_____

Web search and writing

The activities on the next two pages prompt you to share information with a study partner and to search the Web for more information about emergency medical techniques.

Emergency medical techniques

ACTIVITY 9·1

Exchange experiences *Ask your partner the following questions, and add a question of your own.*

1. Have you or anyone in your family ever required emergency medical treatment?

   What happened? _____

   _____

2. Do you know what to do if someone has one of the following medical emergencies?

   ☐ Allergic reaction or anaphylactic shock   ☐ Fractured limb
   ☐ Burn injury   ☐ Heart attack
   ☐ Choking or asphyxia   ☐ Ingestion of poison
   ☐ Electrical shock   ☐ Injury with heavy bleeding
   ☐ Epileptic seizure   ☐ Unconsciousness

3. Your question _____

Discussion *Share your answers with another partner or with the whole group.*

ACTIVITY 9·2

Search the Web *Find information about how to give first aid in the case of a medical emergency, and record the following details. Examples are CPR and the Heimlich maneuver.*

Name of technique   _____

URL   www._____

What to do   _____

_____

_____

_____

Name of technique   _____

URL   www._____

What to do   _____

_____

_____

_____

Name of technique   _____

URL   www._____

What to do   _____

_____

_____

_____

_____

ACTIVITY
9·3

Writing *For a bulletin board at your school, create a poster outlining the steps to take in case of a medical emergency. Be sure to include contact information.*

Cirque du Soleil
A dream makes the big time

Pre-reading

What is your favorite type of entertainment?

☐ Amusement parks
☐ Card and board games
☐ The circus
☐ Computer games
☐ Dances

☐ Live theater
☐ Movies
☐ Music concerts
☐ Sports
☐ Television

☐ _____
☐ _____

Reading text

1   There's always plenty of excitement when the circus comes to town. Painted caravans and loaded tractor trailers roll in, the Big Top goes up, and bright lights and lively music fill the fairgrounds. Since 1871, when P. T. Barnum introduced the first three-ring circus at the Brooklyn World Fair, the traveling circus has captured the imagination of young and old. What girl or boy has not dreamed at least once of running away to join the circus and travel the world? In the case of Guy Laliberté, the dream not only came true, but it has **surpassed** anyone's wildest imagination.

2   Born into a musical family in Quebec, Canada, Laliberté grew up in the right place at the right time. A French-speaking province in a **predominantly** English-speaking country, Quebec has proudly held onto its cultural identity and **nurtured** its artists and performers. The 1960s and 1970s were an explosive era of social change, hippie counterculture, and broad **opportunities** for young people to break out of their parents' mold. As a teenager, Laliberté got his first experience as an impresario by organizing high school events. After graduating, he spread his wings and toured the province as an accordion and harmonica player with a folk group. From there, he traveled to Europe, and when he returned to Canada in 1979 as a musician and fire breather, his search for a job to finance a trip to Florida and Hawaii led him to the artist colony of Baie-Saint-Paul near Quebec City, where stilt walkers, jugglers, dancers, musicians, and fire breathers gathered to perform.

3   In Baie-Saint-Paul, Laliberté teamed up with Daniel Gauthier and Gilles Ste-Croix, who were running a youth hostel for street performers, and formed the Stilt Walkers of Baie-Saint-Paul with local talent. Laliberté **secured** a government grant, and the group was able to tour the province of Quebec in the summer of

1980. Their acrobatic performances were well received by audiences, but they lost money. The following summer, after Laliberté returned from a winter in Hawaii, they added a new act—the Dragon Parade—and ended up breaking even.

4   Encouraged by their success, they organized a street performer festival called La Fête Forain. With Ste-Croix as artistic director, Laliberté as producer, Gauthier as business manager, and Guy Caron, founder of the National Circus School in Montreal, in charge of workshops, plus help from a lot of talented friends, the festival enjoyed runs in three consecutive years and achieved financial success. Laliberté realized the festival's **potential**, and while he was watching the sunset on a beach in Hawaii, the idea of Cirque du Soleil (French for "circus of the sun"), a real circus under a big tent, came to him.

5   The year 1984 marked the 450th **anniversary** of the discovery of Canada by French explorer Jacques Cartier; to celebrate, the government was handing out funding for local events. Laliberté convinced the program manager to support a one-year project to develop a distinctly Québecois circus that would tour 11 towns over three weeks. On June 16, 1984, Le Grand Tour de Cirque du Soleil gave its first performance in the town of Gaspé. In its first year, the newborn circus experienced logistical difficulties and tensions among the artists, but their success with audiences brought everyone together. 1985 was International Youth Year, and further government funding extended the circus project for two more years.

6   The next challenge for Quebec's first home-grown circus was to discover its unique identity. From the very beginning. Cirque du Soleil had been Laliberté's baby, and although he remained the driving force, he also knew how to **harness** the energy of young artists and to **recruit** creative minds. Inspired by European and Chinese theater, Caron and Laliberté began to integrate a storyline into the acrobatic skeleton of the performances. When Laliberté hired Franco Dragone, René Dupère, and Michel Crête, Cirque du Soleil came into its own artistically. As director, Dragone brought his theatrical expertise to the circus and created characters whose story **conveyed** a message to the audience that life could be better and that ordinary people could achieve extraordinary things. To open the show, Dragone had performers enter the tent dressed in trench coats, then **transform** themselves into circus artists. This opening became Cirque du Soleil's trademark.

7   Added to the narrative was Dupère's original musical scores, which created a movielike experience for the audience. Costume designer Crête **departed** entirely **from** the traditional military style of circus costumes by adding color and range to create a distinctive look. Crête also included children in the cast. Together, Dragone and Crête developed shows that had the visual appeal of paintings, and their artistic approach enabled performers to **transcend** language barriers and communicate universal emotions to their audience. The team was able to delight audiences in a way that no other circus had ever done before.

8   Despite its successful artistic innovations, the company was experiencing financial pressures. In 1987, Cirque du Soleil was invited to the Los Angeles Festival. The company had only enough financial resources to get there, but the gamble paid off and Cirque du Soleil became a smash hit. Movie producers, including Columbia Pictures, offered Laliberté partnership deals to make the show into a movie, but he refused to **compromise** the circus's independence and artistic **integrity**. At the end of the year, Cirque du Soleil was debt-free, and by the end of 1988, the company was making a profit. There were setbacks and internal crises, when, for example, Caron and artists loyal to him left, but Laliberté continued to believe in his vision and his team.

9   In 1990, a revolutionary show, *Nouvelle Expérience,* put Cirque du Soleil in the black. It was inspired by Jules Verne's novel about a gold meteor that crashes to earth and scatters a thousand jewels around the planet. After this show, the company never looked back financially, and since then it has achieved unparalleled status in the entertainment business. Cirque du Soleil has expanded from one show to 19 running in more than 270 cities, and it employs more than 5,000 people in 100 different job categories. Its annual revenues are estimated at $810 million. In addition to its international tours, Cirque du Soleil's permanent Las Vegas venue entertains thousands

of visitors every night. Televised versions of Cirque du Soleil's shows have won numerous awards, among them four Primetime Emmys and three Geminis.

10   As a member of Business for Social Responsibility and Business in the Community, Cirque du Soleil has taken its dream beyond entertaining audiences to building community. In 2003, Laliberté set up La TOHU, the City of Circus Arts, in the St-Michel district of Montreal. In addition to making Montreal the center of circus arts, La TOHU operates the biggest environmental urban waste disposal site in North America. In October 2009, Laliberté personally founded the One Drop Foundation, which, in partnership with other nongovernmental organizations, ensures access to clean water and sanitation projects for people in developing countries.

11   The Circus of the Sun has gone beyond one man's idea to become a shining example of the excellence people can achieve when they believe in each other and dream a common dream.

Cirque du Soleil's shows

Show name	Premiere	Theme
Nouvelle Expérience	1990	Performers as jewels spread all around the world
Saltimbanco	1992	Urbanism and a celebration of different cultures living together in mutual respect and harmony
Mystère	1993	The origins of life as told by various mythologies
Alegría	1994	The abuse of power, perseverance, and hope
Quidam	1996	A lonely young girl entertains herself with fantasies of the world of Quidam
O	1998	Water and the arts of the theater
La Nouba	1998	A fairy tale of dreams and reality
Dralion	1999	The fusion of East and West, and harmony between man and nature
Varekai	2002	The Greek myth of Ikarus, who flew too close to the sun on wings made of wax
Zumanity	2003	An exploration of human sensuality
Kà	2004	A story of conflict and love incorporating martial arts
Corteo	2005	A clown observing his own funeral
Delirium	2006	Breaking away from solitude and joining with others to survive
Love	2006	A musical history of the Beatles
Koozå	2007	Solitude and sanctuary
Wintuk	2007	A young boy and his companions in search of snow, which they bring back to their city
Zaia	2008	A young girl's journey of self-discovery through space
Zed	2008	The progression of humanity as seen through the Tarot and its characters
Criss Angel Believe	2008	An exploration of the mind of Criss Angel
Ovo	2009	The mysterious appearance of a giant egg in the insect world

Show name	Premiere	Theme
Banana Shpeel	2009	A vaudeville-based show with slapstick humor
Viva Elvis	2009	The life of rock 'n' roll legend Elvis Presley
Totem	2010	Man's evolution from amphibian to his dream of flying
Zarkana	2011	A magician's loss of his love and his magic, and his appeal to the gods for her return
Iris	2011	A historic look at the movies
Michael Jackson: The Immortal World Tour	2011	A tribute to Michael Jackson, the King of Pop
Amaluna	2012	The queen's daughter's love for one of the young men washed up on the shore of their island

Vocabulary

Organizing vocabulary *Add words and phrases from the reading text that relate to the headings in the two cluster maps that follow. An example has been provided for each cluster map.*

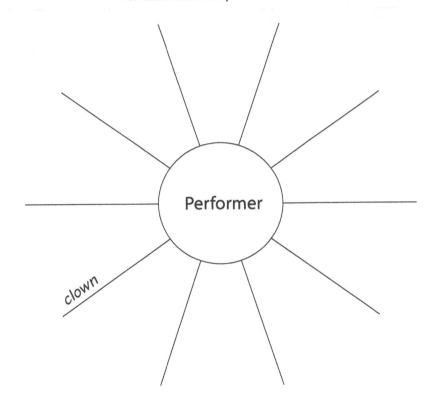

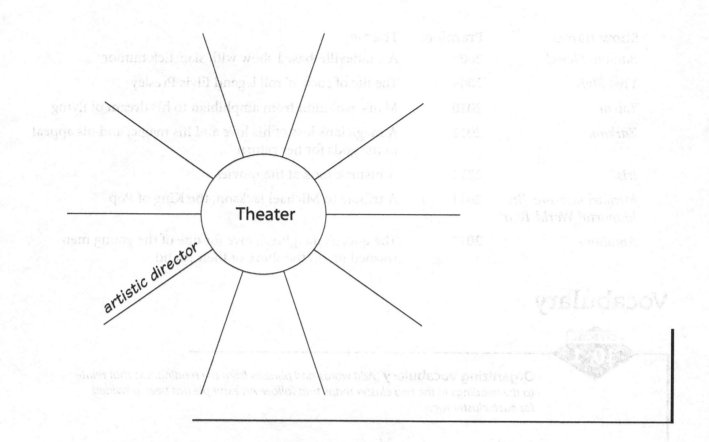

Understanding vocabulary *Each boldface word or phrase is followed by three words or phrases, one of which is unrelated to the others. Indicate the one that doesn't belong.*

1. **anniversary** — celebration — special day — ceremony
2. **compromise** — agreement — argument — trade-off
3. **convey** — confuse — transport — get across
4. **depart from** — change — do differently — carry on
5. **opportunity** — chance — limitation — possibility
6. **harness** — use — release — utilize
7. **integrity** — untruthfulness — honesty — wholeness
8. **nurture** — support — nourish — neglect
9. **potential** — hopelessness — capacity — possibility
10. **predominant** — chief — main — rare
11. **recruit** — dismiss — hire — employ
12. **secure** — guarantee — lose — ensure
13. **surpass** — outdo — exceed — underperform
14. **transcend** — fall back — rise above — beyond
15. **transform** — change — alter — solidify

Using vocabulary *Answer each of the following questions, using the underlined word or phrase in your answer.*

1. In your country, how do married couples celebrate their wedding <u>anniversary</u>?

_____

2. If you want to go to a movie but your friend wants to stay home, how can you <u>compromise</u> so that both of you are happy with the decision?

_____

3. What kind of message do violent video games <u>convey</u> to children who play them?

_____

4. Should teachers always follow their course outline, or is it a good idea once in a while to <u>depart from</u> what is in the textbook?

_____

5. What would be a good <u>opportunity</u> to learn English?

_____

6. Is it possible to <u>harness</u> the sun to provide energy?

_____

7. In which kinds of jobs is it important for people to have <u>integrity</u>?

_____

8. Which abilities and talents should a good school <u>nurture</u>?

_____

9. What do you have the <u>potential</u> to become?

_____

10. What is the <u>predominant</u> language spoken in your part of the country?

_____

11. How do sports teams <u>recruit</u> new players?

_____

12. How can a good education <u>secure</u> a good job for a young person?

_____

13. Have you ever been to a place that <u>surpassed</u> your expectations?

_____

14. If people could <u>transcend</u> their political and cultural differences, what could they achieve?

_____

15. What are some inventions that have <u>transformed</u> our lives?

_____

Reading comprehension

Reading for main ideas *Choose the boldface word or phrase that correctly completes each of the following statements.*

1. The **technical skill** | **creativity** of its artists and directors is what makes Cirque du Soleil so unique and successful.

2. Cirque du Soleil **is** | **isn't** like any other circus in the world.

3. Audiences from different cultures **can** | **can't** understand Cirque du Soleil's performances.

4. Guy Laliberté's dream was to start a new kind of **theater** | **circus**.

5. Right from the beginning, Cirque du Soleil was **artistically successful** | **financially successful.**

6. Teamwork **is** | **isn't** an important part of Cirque du Soleil's success.

7. Cirque du Soleil's shows are based on **acrobatics that entertain the audience** | **stories with characters that deliver a message to the audience.**

8. Music and costumes **are** | **aren't** an integral part of Cirque du Soleil's shows.

9. Cirque du Soleil performs **only in North America** | **all over the world.**

10. Cirque du Soleil **is** | **isn't** involved in projects that build community and protect the environment.

Reading for details *For each of the following sentences, choose the correct answer to fill in the blank.*

1. Guy Laliberté came from a _____ family.
   a. theatrical
   b. musical
   c. business

2. Quebec in the 1960s and 1970s _____ its French-speaking culture and artist-performers.
   a. nurtured
   b. abandoned
   c. didn't care much about

3. Guy Laliberté, Daniel Gauthier, and Gilles Ste-Croix formed a theater group called _____ of Baie-Saint-Paul.
   a. the Stilt Walkers
   b. the Dragon Parade
   c. La Fête Forain

4. In 1981, Laliberté, Ste-Croix, and Guy Caron organized a _____ that ran for three years.
   a. musical festival
   b. film festival
   c. street performer festival

5. On June 16, 1984, Le Grand Tour de Cirque du Soleil gave its first performance in _____.
   a. the capital of Ottawa
   b. the town of Gaspé
   c. the city of Los Angeles

6. Laliberté and Caron got their artistic inspiration from _____.
   a. P. T. Barnum
   b. Broadway
   c. European theater

7. When _____ became artistic director, he brought his expertise in the theater and transformed Cirque du Soleil's shows.
   a. Franco Dragone
   b. René Dupère
   c. Michel Crête

8. Costume designer _____ changed the look of the performers' costumes.
   a. Franco Dragone
   b. René Dupère
   c. Michel Crête

9. Cirque du Soleil's participation in the _____ was a smash hit.
   a. La Fête Forain
   b. Los Angeles Festival
   c. Las Vegas Festival

10. Cirque du Soleil has a permanent venue in _____.
    a. Los Angeles
    b. Montreal
    c. Las Vegas

EXERCISE 10·6

Reading for facts and figures *Match each show name in column 1 with its theme in column 2.*

_____ 1. *O*

_____ 2. *Love*

_____ 3. *Zumanity*

_____ 4. *Iris*

_____ 5. *Nouvelle Expérience*

_____ 6. *Totem*

_____ 7. *Saltimbanco*

_____ 8. *Zed*

_____ 9. *Mystère*

_____ 10. *Dralion*

a. Jewels spread around the world
b. Urbanism and different cultures living together
c. Water
d. Harmony between man and nature
e. Human sensuality
f. The Tarot
g. The origins of life in mythology
h. The Beatles
i. The movies
j. Man's dream of flying

Reading for meaning *Using the information in the statement from the reading text, answer each of the following questions.*

1. "Born into a musical family in Quebec, Canada, Laliberté grew up in the right place at the right time." Was Quebec a good place for young artists and musicians to be born and raised in?
   ☐ Yes
   ☐ No

2. "The 1960s and 1970s were an explosive era of social change, hippie counterculture, and broad opportunities for young people to break out of their parents' mold." Were the 1960s and 1970s a bad time for young people to be different from their parents?
   ☐ Yes
   ☐ No

3. "The following summer, after Laliberté returned from a winter in Hawaii, they added a new act—the Dragon Parade—and ended up breaking even." Did the Stilt Walkers of Baie-Saint-Paul lose money?
   ☐ Yes
   ☐ No

4. "In its first year, the newborn circus experienced logistical difficulties and tensions among the artists, but their success with audiences brought everyone together." Did Cirque du Soleil's success help the artists overcome their problems?
   ☐ Yes
   ☐ No

5. "In 1990, a revolutionary show, *Nouvelle Expérience,* put Cirque du Soleil in the black. It was inspired by Jules Verne's novel about a gold meteor that crashes to earth and scatters a thousand jewels around the planet." Did the new show make the company financially successful?
   ☐ Yes
   ☐ No

Reading skills

Summary *Create a profile of Cirque du Soleil, using the most important details from the reading text.*

The founders _____

Company headquarters _____

Its first performance _____

Important contributors and their roles

_____

_____

_____

_____

_____

_____

Trademark _____

What makes Cirque du Soleil different from other circuses

_____

_____

_____

_____

_____

_____

_____

_____

Awards _____

Number and type of employees _____

Number of running shows and venues _____

Estimated annual revenue _____

Permanent venue _____

Circus arts sponsorship _____

Community building projects

_____

_____

Web search and writing

The activities on the next two pages prompt you to share information with a study partner and to search the Web for more information about Cirque du Soleil's shows.

Cirque du Soleil's amazing shows

ACTIVITY 10·1

Exchange experiences *Ask your partner the following questions, and add a question of your own.*

1. What do you like best about a circus?

☐ Acrobats
☐ Clowns
☐ Dog and pony shows
☐ Elephant acts
☐ Fire breathers and sword swallowers

☐ Jugglers
☐ Magicians
☐ Lion and tiger shows
☐ Tightrope walkers
☐ Trapeze artists

☐ _____

☐ _____

2. Have you ever wanted to run away from home and join the circus? Why or why not?

_____

3. Your question _____

Discussion *Share your answers with another partner or with the whole group.*

ACTIVITY 10·2

Search the Web *Find information on the Internet about some of Cirque du Soleil's shows, and record the information below.*

Name of show _____

URL www._____

Storyline and features _____

_____

_____

_____

Name of show _____

URL www._____

Storyline and features _____

_____

_____

_____

Name of show _____

URL www._____

Storyline and features _____

_____

_____

_____

_____

Writing *Write an outline for a story that you think would make an interesting show for Cirque du Soleil to perform.*

The Findhorn Community
A garden of spirits

Pre-reading

In your opinion, what elements would a paradise on earth contain?

- ☐ Beautiful flower gardens
- ☐ Clear springs and fountains
- ☐ Dense forests
- ☐ Exotic birds
- ☐ Fruit orchards

- ☐ Mountains and valleys
- ☐ Pristine lakes with lots of fish
- ☐ Sunny blue skies
- ☐ Vegetable gardens
- ☐ Wild animals

- ☐ _____
- ☐ _____

Reading text

1   The earth is a showcase of beautiful gardens. The garden at Versailles, France, and the Viceroy's Palace Garden in India were designed as marvels of symmetry. The Butchart Gardens in Victoria, Canada, has become a national historic site and an international tourist attraction. Near Amsterdam, Holland, the Keukenhof Garden displays rainbow rows of tulips. There are gardens of all sizes and configurations, but in one of the most unlikely places on the coast of northern Scotland, only one garden has ever produced 40-pound cabbages and eight-foot delphiniums.

2   In November 1962, Peter and Eileen Caddy and their colleague Dorothy Maclean were fired on short notice and without reason from the four-star hotel where they had been living and working successfully for six years. They accepted their **dismissal**, packed up their belongings, and moved with the Caddys' three small sons into a small touring caravan (a British term for a motor home or RV). Local ordinances **prohibited** camping on the beach beyond the summer season, so with nowhere else to go, the extended family relocated to a small caravan park at Findhorn Bay, near the village of Findhorn, until the spring, they hoped, when hotels would reopen and they would find new employment.

3   Situated next to the unsightly village garbage dump, the Findhorn Bay Caravan Park was one step above homelessness. Gale-force winds blew in regularly from the sea, scattering debris in their paths. All that grew in the surrounding sand and gravel was scruffy gorse, broom, brambles, quitch grass, and a few spiny fir trees. Peter chose a more private and sheltered site for their caravan at the bottom of a hollow, but even this was a far cry from the comforts they had been used to. On their first day at the park, it began to snow. With no job, no money, and no place to go, the group found themselves at the bottom of the barrel.

120

4   Peter, Eileen, and Dorothy, however, were no ordinary people. Peter had a military background, but in his youth he had received training in positive thinking. A highly **intuitive** man, he had come to believe in man's duty to return the planet to a state of love and beauty. Eileen and Dorothy were sensitives,[1] who received spiritual **guidance** while in a state of **meditation**. During the 10 years they had been living and working together, they had come to trust Eileen's and Dorothy's spiritual messages. If they continued to believe in their inner directions and followed them to the letter, all their needs would be met.

5   Their first job was to clean up their living space and transform it with loving **vibrations**. Three months of winter, however, was a long time for a family to be living in close quarters under extreme weather conditions and on limited means. When Peter's unemployment benefits ran out, he collected eight pounds a week in welfare, which was hardly enough for a family to live on. It became clear that they would have to grow a garden, but none of them had gardening experience and nothing **edible** could possibly thrive in the sand.

6   In the spring of 1963, Peter dug three trenches and buried the turf so that it would break down into natural fertilizer. In the nine-by-nine-foot plot, he planted lettuce and radishes. In a second patch, he sowed peas, runner beans, carrots, beets, and lettuce. To get the sandy soil to **absorb** moisture, Peter watered it daily and repeatedly by hand. That spring, Dorothy was told in one of her meditations that she had a job to do, and that was to harmonize with the higher intelligence of nature. The source of her communication, the Devas (*Deva* is Sanskrit for "being of light" or "shining one"), advised her to build compost piles to enrich the soil, which is exactly what Peter did.

7   With no money to buy tools or materials, the novice gardeners were forced to use whatever they could scrounge and collect. As if by magic, assistance started coming their way. In the winter, Eileen had fled the confines of the caravan to meditate at night in a public washroom, and on one occasion her guidance **specified** that they build a patio. One morning, a load of concrete magically turned up in the ditch outside the park gate. When Peter needed straw to cover his compost, a neighbor brought a bale of hay that happened to be lying on the road, and he offered some old lumber that Peter used to build pathways, cold frames, and fences. Neighbors donated horse and sheep manure, and a town shopkeeper gave the Caddys leftover produce. What was too spoiled to eat, they added to their compost.

8   By May, the family was enjoying their first lettuce and radishes. Eileen's guidance had instructed her to **purify** their bodies and absorb cosmic energies by eating less dense and refined foods. Instead of the rich five-course dinners with wine and brandy from their hotel days, they began to consume fruit and garden vegetables with wheat germ, bread, and honey. In addition to their diet, the pure air, sunlight, cold water, hard work, and exercise were doing them good, and they planted leeks, celery, rutabagas, turnips, peas, and more radishes and lettuce.

9   All along, Dorothy maintained contact with the Devas. Overseen by the Landscape Angel, the Devas advised her to think of plants as **divine** and to **radiate** love and appreciation to them. She was given precise growing instructions, and by June, the garden was like nothing anyone had ever seen. Out of the sand grew tall, healthy and abundant vegetables. Their Brussels sprouts reached two feet in height, whereas just across the way, they stopped growing at two or three inches. Their blackberries were the only ones in the entire county to produce fruit.

10   Five years later, 65 different vegetables, 21 kinds of fruit, and more than 40 medicinal and culinary herbs were flourishing in the garden. Beautiful flowers and luscious trees were turning the caravan park into a botanical garden and a major curiosity. Locals flocked to see the wonders that were occurring at the site and to buy surplus produce. Horticulturalists, professional gardeners, members of agricultural societies, lords and ladies—all were at a loss to explain the beauty

---

[1] Here, *sensitive* describes a person who has extrasensory perception and is able to receive messages or sense things that normal human beings are not usually aware of.

and bounty in terms of either traditional horticulture or organic husbandry. Sir George Trevelyan, a respected scholar and educator, was **astonished** at the superior quality of the vegetables and flowers. He could only conclude that something else—Factor X—was at play, and that if Caddy's methods were applied to the Sahara, surely roses would bloom in the desert.

11   Of course, there were critics and skeptics, but the majority of visitors couldn't help but feel the spiritual power of the gardens and its residents. After Peter published a series of pamphlets about the group's experience, people from all walks of life and all over the world came to see and believe, and many stayed. Like the garden, the family expanded into a community,[2] and the caravan park evolved into a New Age center of light. By **embracing** all things and all beings as a part of creation and by cooperating fully with nature, Peter, Eileen, and Dorothy turned a wasteland into an earthly paradise.

12   Although the Caddys have since died—Peter Caddy died in 1994 and Eileen in 2006—the community carries on, 50 years later, as a functioning ecovillage and innovative learning place, and an enduring experiment in **harmonious** living.[3]

Vocabulary

EXERCISE
11·1

Organizing vocabulary *Add words and phrases from the reading text that relate to gardening in the cluster map below. Put verbs on the left, and nouns on the right. Two examples have been provided for the map.*

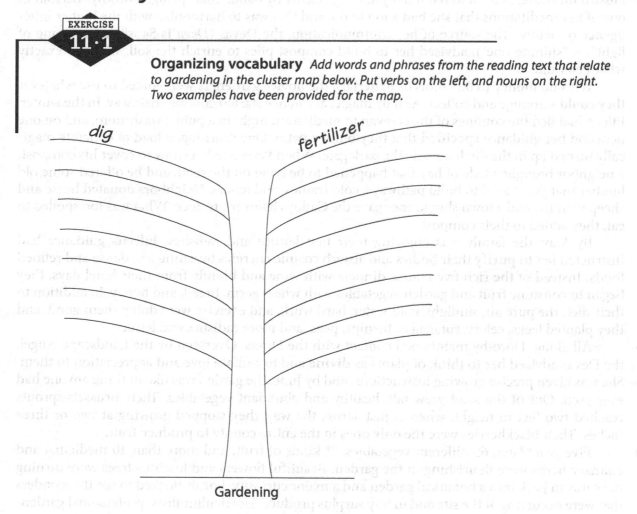

dig   fertilizer

Gardening

---

[2] By 1972, the population had increased to 120 people. Today, more than 320 people and 30 organizations belong to the Findhorn Foundation and Community. The park occupies a 30-acre site, with 300 permanent residents. In 2012, the Findhorn Foundation celebrated its fiftieth anniversary.
[3] Born in 1920, Dorothy Maclean still lives in Findhorn.

Now, add words and phrases from the reading text that relate to spirituality in the cluster map below. An example has been provided for the map.

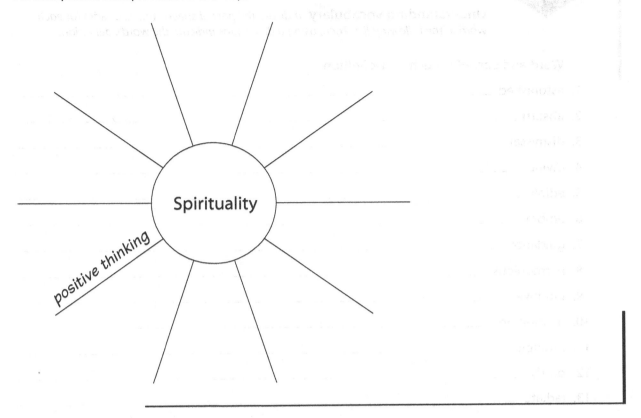

Understanding vocabulary *Indicate the part of speech (n., v., or adj.) for each word in the following list. Then, using a dictionary, indicate the word's definition.*

Word and part of speech **Definition**

1. astonished _____ _____

2. absorb _____ _____

3. dismissal _____ _____

4. divine _____ _____

5. edible _____ _____

6. embrace _____ _____

7. guidance _____ _____

8. harmonious _____ _____

9. intuitive _____ _____

10. meditation _____ _____

11. prohibit _____ _____

12. purify _____ _____

13. radiate _____ _____

14. specify _____ _____

15. vibration[4] _____ _____

Using vocabulary *For each of the following sentences, choose the correct answer to fill in the blank.*

1. If you _____ on a regular basis, it will help you relax and balance your physical, mental, and emotional states.
   a. meditation
   b. meditative
   c. meditate

2. When you put your hand on the machine, you can feel the motor _____.
   a. vibrations
   b. vibrational
   c. vibrating

---

[4]In the context of the reading text, *vibration* is a mood or spiritual atmosphere felt among people.

3. When you have to make a difficult decision, it is sometimes a good idea to trust your
   _____.
   a. intuition
   b. intuitive
   c. intuit

4. When the young actress won the Award for Best Actress, she was _____.
   a. astonishment
   b. astonished
   c. astonish

5. Sometimes, _____ smoking or drinking alcohol without any explanation
   only encourages such behavior in teenagers.
   a. prohibition
   b. prohibited
   c. prohibiting

6. The recipe _____ the ingredients that are needed.
   a. specification
   b. specific
   c. specifies

7. Before people can drink the water from a public water supply, it has to go through
   a process of _____.
   a. purification
   b. pure
   c. purified

8. A sponge _____ water.
   a. absorption
   b. absorbed
   c. absorbs

9. When a plane lands at night, lights on the ground _____ the pilot so that
   he can see the runway.
   a. guidance
   b. guided
   c. guide

10. On her wedding day, the bride looked _____.
    a. radiation
    b. radiant
    c. radiate

11. The employee was _____, because his boss believed that he had stolen
    money from the company.
    a. dismissal
    b. dismissive
    c. dismissed

12. In some cultures, it is common to greet friends with an _____, such as a hug
    or kiss on the cheeks.
    a. embrace
    b. embraced

13. It would be a perfect world if everyone could live together in _____.
    a. harmony
    b. harmonious

14. If you go picking wild mushrooms, you should take a book along in order to identify the _____ ones.
    a. edibility
    b. edible

15. The _____ of Greek and Roman mythology possessed miraculous powers.
    a. divinities
    b. divine

Reading comprehension

Reading for main ideas *Fill in the blanks with information from the reading text.*

1. The Caddys and Dorothy Maclean moved to the caravan park at Findhorn Bay, because
   _____.

2. Peter Caddy decided to plant a garden, because _____
   _____.

3. Their chances of growing a successful garden didn't appear very good, because
   _____.

4. The Caddys and Dorothy Maclean changed their diet, because _____
   _____.

5. When they planted and tended their garden, they followed Dorothy's instructions, because
   _____.

6. Locals and horticulturalists who visited the garden were astonished, because
   _____.

7. Findhorn attracted a community of people from all over the world, because
   _____.

8. The Caddys and Dorothy Maclean turned Findhorn into a paradise, because
   _____.

Reading for details *Rewrite the following sentences, correcting the errors.*

1. Findhorn Bay is located in northern England.

_____

2. The Findhorn Bay Caravan Park was an ideal site for a family to spend the winter.

_____

3. Peter Caddy was a sensitive.

_____

4. Peter Caddy was able to find a job right away in the village of Findhorn to support his family.

_____

_____

5. Peter, Eileen, and Dorothy were experienced gardeners.

_____

6. The family continued to eat the way they had before they moved to Findhorn.

_____

7. Eileen meditated in the caravan when everyone else was asleep.

_____

8. Dorothy made contact with the neighbors, who gave her gardening instructions.

_____

9. Sir George Trevelyan was not impressed with the quality of the Findhorn vegetables and flowers.

_____

_____

10. It took them more than 10 years to establish their garden.

_____

_____

Reading for facts and figures *Answer each of the following questions with information from the reading text.*

1. How big were the cabbages at Findhorn? _____

2. How tall were the delphiniums? _____

3. How high did the Brussels sprouts grow? _____

4. How many kinds of vegetables were grown in the garden? _____

5. How many kinds of fruit were grown? _____

6. How many medicinal and culinary herbs were grown? _____

7. How long has the Findhorn community existed? _____

8. What is the community's current population? _____

Reading for meaning *Indicate whether each of the following statements from the reading text signifies a positive or negative experience for the founders of Findhorn. Then, give the reason for your choice.*

1. "Findhorn Bay Caravan Park was one step above homelessness."
   ☐ Positive
   ☐ Negative

   Reason _____

2. "Even this [more private and sheltered site] was a far cry from the comforts they had been used to."
   ☐ Positive
   ☐ Negative

   Reason _____

3. "As if by magic, assistance started coming their way."
   ☐ Positive
   ☐ Negative

   Reason _____

4. "With no job, no money, and no place to go, the group found themselves at the bottom of the barrel."
   ☐ Positive
   ☐ Negative

   Reason _____

5. "By June, the garden was like nothing anyone had ever seen."
   ☐ Positive
   ☐ Negative

   Reason _____

Reading skills

Summary *Imagine that you are a newspaper or television reporter who is interviewing Dorothy Maclean on the occasion of the 50th anniversary of the Findhorn Community. Write down a list of questions about the most important events in the history of the community.*

EXERCISE
11·8

_____

_____

_____

_____

_____

_____

_____

_____

_____

_____

_____

_____

_____

_____

_____

_____

_____

Web search and writing

The activities on the next two pages prompt you to share information with a study partner and to search the Web for more information about gardening.

Growing a garden

ACTIVITY
11·1

Exchange experiences *Ask your partner the following questions, and add a question of your own.*

1. Do you think it's a good idea to plant your own garden? Why or why not?

   _____

   Have you ever grown a garden or helped someone work in a garden? Describe the experience.

   _____

2. If you were to grow a garden, what would you plant? Write down the different kinds of plants that you would grow.

   Vegetables _____

   Fruit _____

   Berries _____

   Herbs _____

   Flowers _____

3. Your question _____

Discussion *Share your answers with another partner or with the whole group.*

ACTIVITY
11·2

Search the Web *Find tips and advice about how to grow a garden, and record the information below.*

Source of advice   _____

URL   www._____

Main tips   _____

                    _____

                    _____

                    _____

                    _____

Source of advice   _____

URL   www._____

Main tips   _____

_____

_____

Source of advice   _____

URL   www._____

Main tips   _____

_____

_____

ACTIVITY

11·3

Writing *Describe your ideal garden.*

Aron Ralston
Surviving the worst

Pre-reading

How dangerous do you consider the following outdoor sports and activities?

	Not dangerous	Somewhat dangerous	Dangerous	Extremely Dangerous
Alpine skiing	☐	☐	☐	☐
Bungee jumping	☐	☐	☐	☐
Mountain biking	☐	☐	☐	☐
Mountain climbing	☐	☐	☐	☐
Rock climbing	☐	☐	☐	☐
Scuba diving	☐	☐	☐	☐
Skateboarding	☐	☐	☐	☐
Sky diving	☐	☐	☐	☐
Surfing	☐	☐	☐	☐
Whitewater canoeing	☐	☐	☐	☐

Reading text

1   Some people will do anything for fun. They'll climb sheer rock faces or rappel down twisted canyons. They'll dive off cliffs, ski down glaciers, or jump out of airplanes. No mountain is too high, no river too wild, no terrain too rough or rugged.

2   So what makes people risk their necks in out-of-the-way places? Are they bored with life as most people know it? Do they feel more at home in the wilderness than in the city? Are they crazy egomaniacs, or reckless daredevils? Are they addicted to the adrenalin rush? Or do they feel most alive when they're facing death? But what happens when they push their luck, when something goes wrong and they end up in a situation beyond their control? These are questions to which Aron Ralston, thrill-seeker extraordinaire, would know the answers.

3   An honor student with a bright future, Aron graduated from Carnegie Mellon University in Pittsburgh with majors in mechanical engineering and French. He landed a good job as a mechanical engineer with Intel, but he quit after five years and moved to Aspen, Colorado, to be closer to the mountain country he loved. Aron **aspired** to become the first person to climb, alone and in winter, all 59 of Colorado's mountains higher than 14,000 feet. By spring 2003, he had scaled

45 of them, but the melting snow-tops were becoming too treacherous, so he turned to other challenges.

4   On April 26, 2003, 27-year-old Ralston decided to go on a 30-mile circuit of solitary biking and rappelling in the slot canyons[1] of southeastern Utah. He put on a his favorite Phish T-shirt, two pairs of lightweight shorts, running shoes, and thick wool-blend socks. He packed his rappelling gear, a headlamp, headphones, a CD player, extra AA batteries, a digital camera, a mini-digital video camcorder, an imitation Leatherman multitool with pliers and two pocketknife blades, a gallon of water in an insulated hydration pouch, a one-liter plastic water bottle, five chocolate bars, and two burritos. He threw his mountain bike into his truck and drove five hours to Blue John Canyon.[2] He usually left his itinerary with friends, but because he didn't know exactly where he was going, he left a note that said "Utah." He planned to be back home later that night for a party with friends.

5   It was a beautiful day for the "walk in the park" Aron had in mind. He parked his truck at Horseshoe Canyon Trailhead, biked 15 miles to Blue John Canyon Trailhead, and continued on foot. Along the way, he met two young women and spent some time with them exploring the canyon, but at 2 P.M. they parted company. On his last climb of the day through a three-foot-wide slot canyon, he **encountered** a large chockstone the size of a large bus tire wedged between the walls. He kicked at it to test its tightness, then squatted to get a handhold as he lowered himself. While still dangling from the rock, he could feel it shift. He knew he was in trouble. Just as he let go, the boulder slipped and fell. Aron **instinctively** held up his hands to protect himself, but the rock came crashing down, first smashing his left hand, then pinning and crushing his right forearm against the wall. Aron was trapped.

6   At first, he was overcome with disbelief. In a panic, he tried to yank his hand free, but the frantic motion only **intensified** the pain. When the adrenalin and anxiety **subsided**, he began to consider his options:

- Wait and hope someone would come along and get help
- Try to free his hand by chipping away at the rock
- Use his climbing equipment to try to move the rock
- Cut off his arm

7   Not only was Aron in a physical **predicament**, but he had only 500 calories of food and 22 ounces of water that he would have to **ration** to keep himself alive. He made a harness from his climbing equipment so that he could take the weight off his legs and maneuver in the **confines** of the canyon. Unable to sleep, Aron pecked and chipped at the chockstone with his utility knife for the next three days, but he was no match for the rock. Next, he tried to rig his climbing gear to move the boulder, but it wouldn't budge.[3] During the day, sunshine **penetrated** the canyon only enough to warm his lower legs. At night, temperatures dropped so that he shivered and shook with hypothermia. To document what was happening and to share his feelings with his family, Aron videotaped himself. By Tuesday, he ran out of food and water, and **resorted to** drinking his own urine. By Wednesday, the chances of rescue were getting slimmer. Not expecting to survive the night of April 30, he carved his name and the date in the stone wall and recorded a farewell message to his parents.

8   **Deprived** of sleep, Aron hovered between states of lucidity and delirium. In a moment of clarity, he realized that the boulder had been waiting for him all along and that his own choices

---

[1] A slot canyon is formed as flash floods erode hairline cracks in sandstone and form a narrow crevice that twists and turns, making an ideal site for canyoneering.
[2] Blue John Canyon is located in the scenic Robbers Roost area of Utah; it has several miles of narrow slot canyons and desert hiking trails.
[3] Thirteen men with equipment were required to move the 800-pound rock and retrieve Aron's arm.

had led him to where he was. In a hallucinatory state, Aron saw a three-year-old boy playing with a one-armed man. If the boy were his son and if he wanted that vision to come true, there was only one thing he could do. Aron decided to cut off his arm.

9   As early as Sunday, Aron had **contemplated** amputating his arm. The pressure of the rock had immediately cut off the circulation of blood to his hand. Although he could jab his utility knife into the **decomposing** flesh, the blade was too dull to cut through bone. His only alternative now was to break his arm. Under **excruciating** pain, he proceeded to use the boulder as resistance and the weight of his body to snap the bones in his forearm. He then tied the rubber hose from his hydration pack around his arm as a tourniquet, and through waves of pain, he sawed off his arm below the elbow. The amputation took him one hour.

10   Aron wrapped his stump in a plastic grocery bag, made a sling for his arm, and took one last picture of the boulder and his **severed** arm. He then rappelled almost 70 feet down to the bottom of the canyon and hiked five miles in the afternoon heat until he met a Dutch family on vacation. Despite severe dehydration, shock, and the loss of one and a half liters of blood and 40 pounds of body weight, Aron was able to keep on walking in the company of the Dutch man, while the woman and their son managed to attract a search helicopter.[4] Twelve minutes later, and six hours after his amputation, Aron was carried into the hospital at Moab.

11   Few ordeals are as heroic as Aron Ralston's,[5] especially when one considers that since his accident he has returned to Blue John Canyon several times, and he still climbs mountains with a special prosthetic limb. When he goes off by himself, however, Aron leaves an itinerary, the location of his vehicle, and the name of the local sheriff with his family. In addition to pursuing outdoor adventures, he does nonprofit work and is a motivational speaker. He is married, and the father of the boy whose image saved his life.

12   At the end of his book, *Between a Rock and a Hard Place*, Aron wrote that "our purpose as spiritual beings is to follow our bliss, seek our passions, and live our lives as inspiration to others." His story proves him true to his words.

---

[4]When Aron did not show up for work, his co-workers at the mountaineering shop reported him missing. A credit card purchase located him somewhere near Moab, Utah. After an alert for him was issued, someone called the local sheriff's office to say that he had seen Aron's truck. A helicopter was sent to search the area. If it hadn't been for the Dutch woman and son, the pilots would have ended their two-hour search without finding Aron in the canyon.

[5]In 2010, British filmmaker Danny Boyle made the Academy Award–nominated movie *127 Hours*, based on Aron's ordeal.

Vocabulary

Organizing vocabulary *List the words and phrases from the reading text that relate to the following headings. Add the part of speech (n., adj., v., or phr. for phrase) for each word or phrase. An example has been provided for each heading.*

Danger	Outdoor activities	Movement
risk your neck (phr.)	*climbing (n.)*	*dangle (v.)*

EXERCISE
12·2

Understanding and using vocabulary *Complete the following chart with the correct forms of the words from the reading text.*

Noun	Adjective/adverb	Verb
1. confines	_____	_____
2. _____	deprived	_____
3. _____	_____	contemplate
4. _____	_____	intensify
5. _____	_____	penetrate
6. _____	X	aspire
7. _____	decomposing	_____
8. _____	X	encounter
9. _____	X	ration
10. _____	severed	_____
11. _____	instinctive(ly)	X
12. predicament	X	X
13. X	X	resort to
14. X	X	subside
15. X	excruciating	X

EXERCISE
12·3

Understanding and using vocabulary *For each of the following sentences, choose the appropriate word from the chart in Exercise 12-2 as a replacement for the underlined phrase or clause. Be sure to use the correct form of each verb and to pluralize nouns, if necessary.*

1. In order to feed his family, the poor man had to <u>adopt an undesirable course of action</u> by stealing bread.

   _____

2. On our travels, we <u>unexpectedly met</u> many interesting people with fascinating stories.

   _____

3. People living in the slum areas of large cities are <u>suffering a lack</u> of fresh water and sanitation.

   _____

4. When the little girl wandered close to the edge of the swimming pool, her mother rushed toward her <u>without consciously thinking</u> and pulled her back to safety.

   _____

5. When I entered the cave, I was overwhelmed with the smell of a dead animal that had begun <u>to rot</u>.

   _____

6. During the war, the civilian population had to <u>limit the consumption of</u> food, tobacco, and sugar.

   _____

7. The rain came down so hard that it <u>went through</u> our umbrellas.

   _____

8. A migraine headache can be <u>intensely painful</u>.

   _____

9. Despite the doctor's efforts to calm the patient, his anxiety only <u>increased in strength</u>.

   _____

10. The talented young girl <u>has strong ambitions</u> to become a concert violinist.

   _____

11. During the operation, the surgeon had to be careful not to <u>cut off</u> any blood vessels or nerves.

   _____

12. After the traveler discovered that his passport and wallet had been stolen, he found himself in a <u>difficult situation</u>.

   _____

13. A few minutes after I took an aspirin, my headache <u>became less intense</u>.

   _____

14. The prisoner was kept in the <u>enclosed area</u> of a jail cell until his hearing.

   _____

15. Don has been <u>thinking deeply about</u> quitting his job and going back to college to study medicine.

   _____

Reading comprehension

Reading for main ideas *Indicate which of the following statements are true (T) and which are false (F). Indicate why the false statements are false.*

1. _____ Aron Ralston liked to take risks and put himself in dangerous situations.

_____

2. _____ Aron was rescued, because his family and friends knew where he had gone.

_____

3. _____ To free himself, Aron had to cut off his right arm below the elbow.

_____

4. _____ Aron tried every other option before he decided to cut off his arm.

_____

5. _____ Aron considered himself the victim of an accident.

_____

6. _____ Aron was able to survive, because he heard his family's voices.

_____

Reading for details *Number the 13 events below in chronological order.*

_____ He had a vision of a one-armed man playing with a small boy.

_____ The chockstone slipped and trapped Aron's arm.

_____ He cut off his arm.

_____ Aron explored the canyons with two women that he met.

_____ He carved his name and the date in the stone wall.

_____ A rescue helicopter picked him up and took him to the hospital in Moab.

_____ He tried to move the boulder with his climbing gear.

_____ He met a Dutch family, who helped him.

_____ Aron Ralston parked his truck at Horseshoe Canyon Trailhead and biked to Blue John Canyon Trailhead.

_____ He tried to free his arm by chipping at the rock with his utility knife.

_____ He ran out of food and water.

_____ He continued on his own and entered a narrow canyon blocked by a large chockstone.

_____ He wrapped his stump in a plastic bag, made a sling for his arm, and rappelled out of the canyon.

Reading for facts and figures *For each of the following sentences, choose the correct answer to fill in the blank.*

1. Aron Ralston's ordeal took place in _____.
   a. Arizona
   b. Colorado
   c. Utah

2. He was trapped in a slot canyon for _____ days.
   a. four
   b. five
   c. six

3. The boulder that crushed his hand weighed _____ pounds.
   a. 8
   b. 80
   c. 800

4. When he got trapped, he had only _____ calories of food.
   a. 100
   b. 500
   c. 1,000

5. It took him _____ to amputate his arm.
   a. one hour
   b. two hours
   c. three hours

6. During his ordeal, he lost _____ pounds.
   a. 4
   b. 14
   c. 40

7. After amputating his arm, he lost _____ liter/liters of blood.
   a. one half
   b. one and a half
   c. two

8. He had to hike _____ miles before he found help.
   a. four
   b. five
   c. six

9. He arrived at the hospital _____ hours after he had amputated his arm.
   a. four
   b. five
   c. six

10. Aron _____ about his experience.
    a. wrote a book
    b. made a movie
    c. posted a blog

Reading for meaning *For each of the following pairs of sentences, choose the boldface phrase in the second sentence that supports the first sentence.*

1. "It was a beautiful day for the 'walk in the park' Aron had in mind."

   Aron thought that climbing in Blue John Canyon **would be** | **wouldn't be** easy.

2. "While still dangling from the rock, he could feel it shift. He knew he was in trouble."

   Aron **had a feeling** | **didn't have a feeling** that something bad was going to happen to him.

3. "Unable to sleep, Aron pecked and chipped at the chockstone with his utility knife for the next three days, but he was no match for the rock."

   Aron | **The rock** was the winner in the struggle.

4. "In a moment of clarity, he realized that the boulder had been waiting for him all along and that his own choices had led him to where he was."

   Aron **took responsibility** | **didn't take responsibility** for his predicament.

5. "As early as Sunday, Aron had contemplated amputating his arm. The pressure of the rock had immediately cut off the circulation of blood to his hand."

   Aron knew that his arm **could be saved** | **couldn't be saved**.

6. "At the end of his book, *Between a Rock and a Hard Place,* Aron wrote that 'our purpose as spiritual beings is to follow our bliss, seek our passions, and live our lives as inspiration to others'."

   Paraphrase the quotation.

   _____

   _____

Reading skills

Retelling the story *Imagine that you are Aron Ralston and are keeping a diary of the events that took place in Blue John Canyon. The first entry has been provided for each time period.*

Saturday morning, April 26

Am up bright and early and ready for my trip to Utah. Should be fun.

_____

Saturday afternoon, April 26

I'm in big trouble.

_____

Sunday, April 27

Thought about cutting off my arm, but there's no way I can do it.

_____

Monday, April 28

Have been trying to chip away enough of the boulder to free my arm, but no luck!

_____

Tuesday, April 29

Am out of food and water.

_____

Wednesday, April 30

I did it!

_____

Web search and writing

The activities on the next two pages prompt you to share information with a study partner and to search the Web for more information about survival stories.

Survival stories

ACTIVITY 12·1

Exchange experiences *Ask your partner the following questions, and add a question of your own.*

1. Have you ever been in a dangerous situation? What do you think you would do if you got lost or trapped in a place and no one knew your whereabouts?

_____

2. What devices and equipment should you carry with you when you travel or go to a remote area?

☐ A cell phone   ☐ A flashlight
☐ A change of clothing   ☐ An army knife
☐ A compass   ☐ Food
☐ A digital camera   ☐ Matches
☐ A first-aid kit   ☐ Water

☐ _____   ☐ _____

3. Your question _____

Discussion *Share your answers with another partner or with the whole group.*

ACTIVITY 12·2

Search the Web *Find stories of people who have survived dangerous situations, such as airplane crashes, shipwrecks, earthquakes and other natural disasters, and strange accidents. Record the following information.*

Name of survivor _____

URL   www._____

What happened   _____

                    _____

                    _____

                    _____

Name of survivor _____

URL www._____

What happened _____

_____

_____

Name of survivor _____

URL www._____

What happened _____

_____

_____

_____

_____

ACTIVITY
12·3

Writing *Create a list of tips on what people should do if they find themselves in a situation where they are lost or injured.*

Harry Potter
More than magic

Pre-reading

When you were a child, what kinds of stories did you like?

- ☐ Adventure stories
- ☐ Animal stories
- ☐ Detective stories
- ☐ Fairy tales
- ☐ Real-life stories

- ☐ Scary stories
- ☐ Science fiction stories
- ☐ Superhero stories
- ☐ Stories about foreign countries
- ☐ Stories with a message

☐ _____

☐ _____

Did your parents read stories to you when you were a child? _____

Is it important for children to read books? Why or why not?

_____

_____

Reading text

1   The list of beloved children's books is long: *Grimm's Fairy Tales*, *Winnie the Pooh*, *Alice in Wonderland*, *The Tale of Peter Rabbit*, *Charlotte's Web*, *The Cat in the Hat*, *Charlie and the Chocolate Factory*, *Heidi*, to name but a few. As delightful and entertaining, as moving and inspirational as all of them are, none can work the magic of J. K. Rowling's *Harry Potter*.

2   Harry Potter, the orphan **wizard** and star of the seven-book series by J. K. Rowling, came into the world in 1990 on a commuter train traveling between Manchester and London, England. As 25-year-old Joanne Rowling stared out the window, she imagined an unnamed boy wizard who didn't know he was a wizard and who went off to wizard school. Joanne had been writing for herself since childhood, and now she had the beginnings of a story that would take her to the top of best-seller lists and make her a famous writer.

3   The idea for *Harry Potter and the Philosopher's Stone* came suddenly, but it would take Joanne five years to complete it. Between moving to Portugal in 1991 to teach English and returning with her infant daughter to Britain at the end of 1993, she had produced only pages of notes and the first three chapters. She settled in Edinburgh, Scotland, and with no job prospects and only social assistance to **rely on**, she went to work on her book. The first two publishers to whom she sent her manuscript **rejected** it, but luckily she found a literary agent to represent her at Christopher Little Agency.

4   Christopher Little sent Joanne's manuscript to nine publishers, only to receive nine rejections. At the time, children's books about sports and ponies were in. Lengthy fantasy books by a first-time author about boy wizards, boarding schools, witchcraft, darkness, and evil were out. Nevertheless, Christopher Little passed the manuscript on to Barry Cunningham, the children's editor at Bloomsbury Publishing, who was **scouting around** at the Frankfurt Book Fair for books that children would **cherish** like their favorite stuffed animal. He and his eight-year-old daughter loved *Harry Potter and the Philosopher's Stone*, and in August 1996, Bloomsbury offered Joanne Rowling a modest publishing deal. At last, she was going to see her book in print, but first she was advised to shorten it, make some minor changes, and change her name from Joanne to J. K. (the *K* after her grandmother Kathleen) Rowling so that she wouldn't be taken as a writer of girls' books. *Harry Potter and the Philosopher's Stone* was scheduled for release in June 1997, but with no great expectations of making very much money on her book, Joanne received an £8,000 grant from the Scottish Arts Council to support herself and begin a second book.

5   In the UK, *Harry Potter and the Philosopher's Stone* was an **unanticipated** success, going into a second printing four days after its release on June 26, 1997.[1] One year later, sales hit 70,000 copies. In 1997, the book won a gold award in the Nestlé Smarties Book Prize and the Children's Book of the Year Award at the British Book Awards, as well as the FCBG and Cable Children's Book Awards. The first children's book to make it to the top of the *London Times* best-seller list, *Harry Potter and the Philosopher's Stone* was becoming so popular with adults that Bloomsbury brought out a special adult edition. In June 1998, translated versions appeared in France, Germany, Italy, Holland, Greece, Finland, and Denmark.

6   In April 1997, Arthur A. Levine of Scholastic Publications won the American publishing rights to Joanne's book at an auction organized by Christopher Little. Released on September 1, 1998 under the title *Harry Potter and the Sorcerer's Stone*, the American version was quickly finding fans. *Harry Potter* hadn't yet made its way into chain booksellers, but independent bookstores were enthusiastically selling and **promoting** the book by word of mouth. Reviews were sparse, but hugely favorable. By mid-December, there were 100,000 books in print in the United States alone, and by the end of the month, *Harry Potter and the Sorcerer's Stone* hit No. 16 on the prestigious *New York Times* Best Seller list, where it remained for six months and climbed to No. 4.

7   With the Internet taking off between 1998 and 1999, Harry Potter mania spread like wildfire through chat rooms, message boards, social networks, blogs, and a **proliferation** of fan-run and fan fiction websites. Fans were turning into fanatics. Three months before the release of the second book, *Harry Potter and the Chamber of Secrets*,[2] impatient devotees were preordering with new online retailer Amazon.com at such a rate that Scholastic moved its publishing date forward by two months in order to avoid a price war. When *Harry Potter and the Goblet of Fire* was simultaneously **launched** in the UK and US at midnight on July 8, 2000, kids and parents showed up in Harry Potter costumes complete with glasses and scars painted on their foreheads.

8   Harry Potter was taking the world by storm. When *Harry Potter and the Chamber of Secrets* came out on July 2, 1999, it sold its first run of 250,000 copies and hit No. 1 on the *New York Times* Best Seller list, a first for a children's book. In the UK, *Chamber of Secrets* stayed No. 1 in adult best-seller charts for a month after publication. After *Harry Potter and the Prisoner of Azkaban* **debuted** to international **acclaim**, the three books occupied the top three best-seller spots on the *New York Times* Best Seller list for 80 weeks, **outpacing** such popular authors as John Grisham, Nora Roberts, and Isabel Allende. Global sales for the first two books swelled from one million to 75 million, and after *Prisoner of Azkaban* came out, sales skyrocketed to 325 million.

---

[1] The source for these and the following sales figures is Melissa Annelli's *Harry, A History: The True Story of a Boy Wizard, His Fans, and Life inside the Harry Potter Phenomenon* (New York: Pocket Books, 2008).
[2] *Harry Potter and the Chamber of Secrets* would also win a second Nestlé Smarties Book Prize and make J. K. Rowling the first author to win two years in a row. She would top that record with a third Smarties award for her third book, *Harry Potter and the Prisoner of Azkaban*.

9   Each book outdid the previous one in sales. *Harry Potter and the Goblet of Fire* came out in the UK with a first print run of one million copies and broke all records for first-day sales. Published in Britain, the US, Canada, and Australia at the same time, the fifth book, *Harry Potter and the Order of the Phoenix,* became the fastest-selling book in history. In the first 24 hours, *Harry Potter and the Half-Blood Prince* sold nine million copies, and *Harry Potter and the Deathly Hallows,* the last and the hottest, sold 15 million in one day. Since its debut in 1997, the seven-book series has been translated into 67 languages and total global sales are estimated at $450 million.

10   The Harry Potter **phenomenon** has gone beyond the page. In 1998, the first movie rights were sold to Warner Brothers for £1 million, and all eight films have been top box-office hits. In addition to the big-screen experience, fans can take part in the Wizarding World of Harry Potter, which opened in Orlando, Florida, on June 18, 2010, as part of Universal Parks and Resorts' Islands of Adventure theme park. In December 2011, Universal Studio announced plans for a second park in Los Angeles, which is scheduled to open in 2016. *Harry Potter* has also **spawned** up to 400 products, including video games, playing cards, clothing, and toys. Apart from its commercial success, the series has been credited with getting children interested in reading again and with helping them improve their reading skills.

11   In the short span of five years, Joanne Rowling went from an unknown, unemployed, single mother to one of the most successful and popular children's authors of all times. According to the *Sunday Times Rich List,* J. K. Rowling is the twelfth-richest woman in Great Britain.[3] Her first American tour was a nonevent, but following the publication of *Harry Potter and the Prisoner of Azkaban,* an average of 750 to 1,000 fans showed up for 30 signings in eight cities. In Worcester, Massachusetts, organizers planned for 200 people, but were overwhelmed with an onslaught of 2,000. Not since the arrival of the Beatles in 1964 had anyone from Britain been greeted with such adoration. For her service to children's literature, she received the Order of the British Empire in 2001.

12   In her fertile imagination, J. K. Rowling succeeded in creating spellbinding stories and lovable characters with amazing magical powers. What is even more amazing is that in her wildest dreams, she could never have **envisioned** how powerful Harry Potter's magic would become.

Book release dates and sales[4]

Title	UK release	US release	Sales (millions of copies)
Harry Potter and the Philosopher's/Sorcerer's Stone	June 26, 1997	September 1, 1998	107
Harry Potter and the Chamber of Secrets	July 2, 1998	July 2, 1999	60
Harry Potter and the Prisoner of Azkaban	July 8, 1999	September 1, 1999	55
Harry Potter and the Goblet of Fire	July 8, 2000	July 8, 2000	55
Harry Potter and the Order of the Phoenix	June 21, 2003	June 21, 2003	55
Harry Potter and the Half-Blood Prince	July 16, 2005	July 16, 2005	65
Harry Potter and the Deathly Hallows	July 21, 2007	July 21, 2007	44

[3] In 2000, J. K. Rowling established Volant, a charitable trust that undertakes projects to deal with poverty and social issues. Since that time, she has also supported Gingerbread, an organization that acts as an advocate for single parents.
[4] From "How Stuff Works," http://entertainment.howstuffworks.com/arts/literature/20-best-selling-childrens-books19.htm.

Movie release dates and box office receipts[5]

Title	Year of release	Gross (worldwide)
Harry Potter and the Philosopher's/Sorcerer's Stone	2001	$ 974,755,371
Harry Potter and the Chamber of Secrets	2002	878,979,634
Harry Potter and the Prisoner of Azkaban	2004	796,688,549
Harry Potter and the Goblet of Fire	2005	896,911,078
Harry Potter and the Order of the Phoenix	2007	939,885,929
Harry Potter and the Half-Blood Prince	2009	934,416,487
Harry Potter and the Deathly Hallows (Part One)	2010	956,399,711
Harry Potter and the Deathly Hallows (Part Two)	2011	1,328,111,219

Vocabulary

EXERCISE
13·1

Organizing vocabulary *On the book cover below, list 10 words from the reading text that relate to popularity.*

---

[5] From "Box Office Mojo," http://boxofficemojo.com/franchises/chart/?id=harrypotter.htm.

On the lefthand page below, list 10 words from the reading text that relate to books. On the righthand page, list 10 words that relate to publishing.

Understanding vocabulary *Indicate the part of speech (n., v., or adj.) for each boldface word or phrase below. Each is followed by three words or phrases, one of which means the opposite of the others. Indicate the antonym.*

1. **acclaim** _____	praise	criticism	approval
2. **cherish** _____	dislike	love	treasure
3. **debut** _____	first appear	lead off	finish
4. **envision** _____	not see	imagine	foresee
5. **launch** _____	start	introduce	cancel
6. **outpace** _____	run behind	outdo	go faster
7. **reject** _____	give back	refuse	accept
8. **rely on** _____	depend on	do without	count on
9. **phenomenon** _____	rare occurrence	sensation	everyday event
10. **proliferation** _____	large number	rapid growth	small amount
11. **promote** _____	publicize	neglect	market
12. **scout around** _____	find immediately	look for	hunt for
13. **spawn** _____	generate	breed	destroy
14. **unanticipated** _____	unexpected	known	unbelievable
15. **wizard** _____	magician	sorcerer	normal person

EXERCISE 13·3

Using vocabulary *Complete each of the following sentences with the appropriate word from the list in Exercise 13-2. Be sure to use the correct form of each verb and to pluralize nouns, if necessary.*

1. The television show *The X-Files* _____ an interest in the existence of UFOs.

2. Toward the end of the race, the marathon runner was able to _____ last year's winner and set a new record.

3. When I was a child, I _____ my favorite teddy bear and slept with it every night.

4. In the field of entertainment, Cirque du Soleil has become an international

   _____.

5. My brother is a real math _____. He can solve difficult problems even faster than the teacher.

6. Toyota _____ its hybrid car, the Prius, in 1997.

7. When I decided to buy a new laptop, I first went to different electronics stores and

   _____ for the best deal.

8. The university _____ applications from students whose GPA is below 2.0.

9. The rock band's new CD met with positive critical _____.

10. A lot of interesting international films _____ at last year's Cannes Film Festival.

11. World leaders should do more to _____ international cooperation and world peace.

12. Nowadays, most people _____ the Internet as their main source of information.

13. In *The Lord of the Rings,* J. R. R. Tolkien _____ an imaginary place called Middle Earth.

14. The school drama club's performance of *A Midsummer Night's Dream* was an

    _____ hit with parents and students.

15. During the Cold War, the _____ of nuclear weapons posed a real threat to world peace.

Reading comprehension

Reading for main ideas *Match each of the following headlines with the corresponding paragraph of the reading text.*

a. Harry Potter and the Philosopher's Stone *a Success in UK, Wins Awards*
b. *The Harry Potter Phenomenon Spawns Movies, Amusement Park, Numerous Products*
c. *J. K. Rowling's* Harry Potter *Series Most Magical of Children's Books*
d. *Fans Go Crazy over Harry Potter, Books' Popularity Spreads like Wildfire*
e. *Unemployed Single Mother's Book Rejected by Publishers*
f. *Global Sales Skyrocket, Each Book Outselling the Last*
g. *Literary Agent Helps Joanne Rowling Get Publishing Offer from Bloomsbury*
h. Harry Potter *Sets Sales Records and Goes International*
i. *American Edition Published by Scholastic Publications Gets Off to Slow Start, But Soon Hits New York Times Best Seller List*
j. *J. K. Rowling Becomes a Media Superstar*
k. *Harry Potter Has More than Magic*
l. *Harry Potter Story Comes to Unknown Writer on Commuter Train*

_____ Paragraph 1

_____ Paragraph 2

_____ Paragraph 3

_____ Paragraph 4

_____ Paragraph 5

_____ Paragraph 6

_____ Paragraph 7

_____ Paragraph 8

_____ Paragraph 9

_____ Paragraph 10

_____ Paragraph 11

_____ Paragraph 12

Reading for details *Indicate which of the following statements are true (T) and which are false (F). Indicate why the false statements are false.*

1. _____ Joanne Rowling thought up the story of Harry Potter while she was teaching English in Portugal.

_____

2. _____ *Harry Potter and the Philosopher's Stone* was the first thing Joanne Rowling had ever written.

_____

3. _____ She couldn't find a publisher for her book, but she found a literary agent who was willing to represent her.

_____

4. _____ Publishers weren't interested in her book, because stories about wizards and boarding schools weren't popular at the time.

_____

5. _____ It was Joanne Rowling's idea to change her name to J. K. Rowling to prevent boys from thinking that she wrote books only for girls.

_____

6. _____ Sales of *Harry Potter and the Philosopher's Stone* hit 70,000 in the first week.

_____

7. _____ *Harry Potter and the Philosopher's Stone* won three awards in the same year it was published.

_____

8. _____ J. K. Rowling's books didn't sell as well in the US as they did in the UK, because she was a British writer.

_____

9. _____ The Internet created a lot of publicity for the *Harry Potter* series.

_____

10. _____ Three *Harry Potter* books were on the *New York Times* Best Seller list at the same time.

_____

11. _____ *Harry Potter* books were never popular with adults.

_____

12. _____ Each new *Harry Potter* book sold more copies than the previous one.

_____

13. _____ *Harry Potter* books have been popular only in English-speaking countries.

_____

14. _____ J. K. Rowling's first signing tour in the US was a huge success.

_____

15. _____ *Harry Potter and the Deathly Hallows* was the last book in the series and was the biggest seller on the day of its release.

_____

_____

EXERCISE

13·6

Reading for facts and figures *Match each of the statements below with one of the following book/movie titles. Some titles may be used more than once.*

a. *Harry Potter and the Philosopher's Stone*
b. *Harry Potter and the Chamber of Secrets*
c. *Harry Potter and the Prisoner of Azkaban*
d. *Harry Potter and the Goblet of Fire*
e. *Harry Potter and the Order of the Phoenix*
f. *Harry Potter and the Half-Blood Prince*
g. *Harry Potter and the Deathly Hallows*

1. _____ has sold more than 44 million copies.

2. _____ was the first children's book to reach the top of the *London Times* best-seller list.

3. _____ was launched at midnight on the same day in the UK and the US.

4. _____ was the first children's book to reach No. 1 on the *New York Times* Best Seller list.

5. _____ was translated into seven languages in 1998.

6. _____ appeared on the *New York Times* Best Seller list along with the first two books for a period of 80 weeks.

7. _____ became the fastest-selling book in history.

8. _____ sold nine million copies on the first day of its release.

9. _____ was made into a two-part movie.

10. _____ made more money at the box office than any other movie except *Harry Potter and the Deathly Hallows*.

EXERCISE
13·7

Reading for meaning *Indicate whether each of the following statements from the reading text shows that the* Harry Potter *books and J. K. Rowling were already or not yet popular.*

1. "Lengthy fantasy books by a first-time author about boy wizards, boarding schools, witchcraft, darkness, and evil were out."
   a. Already popular
   b. Not yet popular

2. "And now she had the beginnings of a story that would take her to the top of best-seller lists."
   a. Already popular
   b. Not yet popular

3. "With no great expectations of making very much money on her book, Joanne received an £8,000 grant from the Scottish Arts Council to support herself and begin a second book."
   a. Already popular
   b. Not yet popular

4. "Three months before the release of the second book, *Harry Potter and the Chamber of Secrets,* impatient devotees were preordering with new online retailer Amazon.com at such a rate that Scholastic moved its publishing date forward by two months in order to avoid a price war."
   a. Already popular
   b. Not yet popular

5. "*Harry Potter* hadn't yet made its way into chain booksellers."
   a. Already popular
   b. Not yet popular

6. "Harry Potter was taking the world by storm."
   a. Already popular
   b. Not yet popular

7. "Her first American tour was a nonevent."
   a. Already popular
   b. Not yet popular

8. "The Harry Potter phenomenon has gone beyond the page."
   a. Already popular
   b. Not yet popular

Reading skills

EXERCISE
13·8

Summary *Write an article for your school newspaper with the headline* Unemployed Single Mother Becomes Famous Author. *Your article about J. K. Rowling and the Harry Potter success story should be 300 to 350 words long. Be sure to make an outline of the most important events and details before you begin writing. Your story should include the following.*

- *Background information about Joanne Rowling and how she got the idea for her first book*
- *How her book came to be published in the UK and the US*
- *The success and popularity of her books*
- *The Harry Potter phenomenon: movies, an amusement park, and hundreds of products for fans*

Web search and writing

The activities on the next two pages prompt you to share information with a study partner and to search the Web for more information about popular children's books.

The magical world of children's books

ACTIVITY 13·1

Exchange experiences *Ask your partner the following questions, and add a question of your own.*

1. Which *Harry Potter* books have you read, and which *Harry Potter* movies have you seen?

   ☐ *Harry Potter and the Philosopher's/Sorcerer's Stone*
   ☐ *Harry Potter and the Chamber of Secrets*
   ☐ *Harry Potter and the Prisoner of Azkaban*
   ☐ *Harry Potter and the Goblet of Fire*
   ☐ *Harry Potter and the Order of the Phoenix*
   ☐ *Harry Potter and the Half-Blood Prince*
   ☐ *Harry Potter and the Deathly Hallows*

   Which is your favorite? _____

2. Which of the following children's books have you read or heard of?

   ☐ *The Adventures of Tom Sawyer*   ☐ *Heidi*
   ☐ *Alice in Wonderland*   ☐ *The Tale of Peter Rabbit*
   ☐ *The Cat in the Hat*   ☐ *Where the Wild Things Are*
   ☐ *Charlie and the Chocolate Factory*   ☐ *Winnie the Pooh*
   ☐ *Charlotte's Web*   ☐ *The Wizard of Oz*

3. Your question _____

Discussion *Share your answers with another partner or with the whole group.*

ACTIVITY 13·2

Search the Web *Find interesting children's books, and record the following information.*

Name of book and author   _____

URL   www._____

Characters and storyline   _____

_____

_____

_____

Name of book and author _____

URL www._____

Characters and storyline _____

_____

_____

_____

_____

Name of book and author _____

URL www._____

Characters and storyline _____

_____

_____

_____

ACTIVITY
13·3

Writing *Create a plot summary for a children's book. Where does the story take place? Who are the characters? What happens? Is there an element of magic in your story?*

The Paralympics
Believe in yourself

Pre-reading

Which of the following sports or games interest you?

☐ Basketball
☐ Biathlon
☐ Equestrian dressage
☐ Figure skating
☐ Gymnastics
☐ Hockey

☐ Rowing
☐ Skiing
☐ Soccer/football
☐ Swimming
☐ Tennis

Reading text

1   Since 1896, the Olympic Games have celebrated achievement in sports by the world's top athletes on a four-year cycle. Opening with fanfare on a Friday and ending three Sundays later, the Olympics and its medalists **dominate** television, newspapers, and conversations. After the joy and drama surrounding record setters and record breakers, the closing ceremony of the Olympics seems anticlimactic—unless we look beyond and into the shadows where athletes show what they are really made of during the world's second biggest international **elite** sporting event, the Paralympics.

History of the Paralympics

2   The first official sports **competition** for athletes with disabilities was held on July 29, 1948, the opening day of the Olympic Games in London, England, with 16 ex-servicemen and servicewomen competing at archery. The International Wheelchair Games were organized by Dr. Ludwig Guttmann, a German-Jewish neurologist who had emigrated to England in 1939. Dr. Guttmann first conducted research into spinal cord injuries at the Nuffield Department of Neurosurgery in Oxford, and in 1944, he established the Stoke Mandeville Hospital in Aylesbury to **rehabilitate** injured war veterans and civilians. This "father of sport for people with disabilities" **advocated** the power of sports **therapy** to develop his patients' physical strength and sense of self-worth, as well as to **enrich** their quality of life.

3   In 1952, the Stoke Mandeville Games were **expanded** to include Dutch ex-servicemen. The International Stoke Mandeville Games continued in Rome until 1960, when Dr. Guttmann's games were officially recognized as the Paralympic[1]

---

[1] *Para* means "beside" or "alongside" in Greek.

Games, making his dream of an international sports event for athletes with **impairments** a reality. In Rome, 400 athletes from 23 countries **participated**, and from there the Paralympic Games took off. The Paralympic Winter Games debuted in Örnsköldsvik, Sweden, in 1976. Since the 1992 Winter Games in Albertville, France, and the 1998 Summer Games in Seoul, South Korea, the Paralympics have shared venues with the Olympic Games. In the 2008 Summer Paralympic Games in Beijing, 4,011 athletes (including 1,383 women) from 146 countries took part in 20 sports and 472 events. In the 2010 Winter Paralympics in Vancouver, 502 athletes from 44 countries competed in 5 sports and 64 events. In the 2012 Summer Paralympics in London, 4,250 athletes from 164 countries competed in 20 sports and 503 medal events.

Disabilities and impairment

4   Since September 22, 1989, the Paralympics have been overseen by the International Paralympic Committee (IPC), an international nonprofit organization with headquarters in Düsseldorf, Germany. Over the years, the Paralympics have broadened their scope from athletes in wheelchairs to athletes with physical, visual, and intellectual disabilities. These fall under six categories.

1. **Amputees** are missing a limb or part of a limb as a result of a congenital defect, an accident, or a medical condition such as cancer or diabetes.
2. Due to **spinal cord injuries**, paraplegics cannot use their legs or the muscles of the lower body and are confined to wheelchairs.
3. Athletes with **cerebral palsy** can control neither their facial and limb movements nor their speech. Cerebral palsy results from a critical lack of oxygen to a baby's brain before, during, or after birth.
4. Athletes with **visual impairment** may have partial sight or be completely blind.
5. Athletes with **intellectual impairment** have disabilities due to a congenital defect, an accident, or a medical condition. The International Special Olympic Games, held independently every two years, were set up specifically for children and adults with severe intellectual disabilities.
6. **Les Autres** refers to other physical disabilities, including multiple sclerosis, muscular dystrophy, spina bifida, polio, dwarfism, and certain congenital deformities.

5   In each of the six categories, competitors are **classified** according to their level of disability. This classification system ensures fairness in competition and encourages a large number of participants. Until the 1980s, a medical **evaluation** determined an athlete's level of impairment. The system was later altered to focus on the athlete's ability to demonstrate the skills **required** in the particular event rather than on the medical disability. For example, as long as leg amputees can perform with equal functionality, they can compete against each other regardless of the reason for the loss of their legs. Classifiers with specialized medical and technical knowledge carry out the evaluation. To qualify for competition, athletes must also take part in world championships and achieve set time limits for performance. Hockey players, for example, have to show commitment to the game as well as physical skill.

Paralympic events

6   There are 20 sports in the summer games and 5 in the winter games, each broken down into individual events. Some traditional sports events have been **modified** to **accommodate** various disabilities and impairments, while others have been specially created. Some examples follow.

- ◆ **Athletics** The 18 traditional track, throwing, jumping, marathon, and pentathlon events are the largest category. Blind and partially sighted athletes, for example, are allowed to run with a guide runner in events up to 400 meters, and with two guide runners for longer distances. For amputees, special prostheses and other adaptive devices are allowed.

- **Goalball** Designed for the visually impaired, goalball is played by teams of six players, with three on the court at a time. The object of the game is to score the most goals by rolling a hollow rubber ball containing bells into the opponent's net. Players, who kneel or lie on the floor, must wear masks.
- **Football-7-a-side** Athletes with cerebral palsy or neurological impairments play this variation of soccer. A team of seven plays on a smaller field with smaller nets, and there are no offside penalties.
- **Ice sledge hockey** Invented in Sweden, this Paralympic variation on ice hockey has been included in the winter games since 1994. Players move across the ice on a metal sled with blades and carry two sticks, equipped with a pick on one end and a blade on the other. The game is open to athletes with cerebral palsy, multiple sclerosis, spinal injury, double-leg amputation, or any impairment that confines them to a wheelchair or that limits their mobility to short distances.
- **Skiing** Skiers with disabilities affecting both legs can use a sit-ski. Small skis, called outriggers, are attached to the ski poles for balance and maneuverability.
- **Biathlon** The athlete's rifle is adapted to pick up a frequency from a transmitter located in the target's center. The closer the shooter's aim, the higher the frequency's pitch.
- **Wheelchair events** Paraplegics and Les Autres confined to a wheelchair can compete in archery, dance, fencing, tennis, table tennis, volleyball, basketball, rugby, and curling.

Paralympic heroes

7   To qualify for the Paralympics, athletes require not only tremendous dedication, fortitude, and support from their families and trainers, but also financial backing to follow their dreams. Paralympic medalists are not as heavily supported by their governments—or as publicly celebrated—as their Olympic counterparts. The following incomplete list confirms how deserving Paralympians are of admiration and recognition.

- **Trischa Zorn** of the United States, who was born blind, holds the record as the most successful Paralympic athlete. Competing in blind swimming events from 1980 to 2004, she has won 55 medals, 41 of which are gold.
- **Ragnhild Myklebust** of Norway, with one leg amputated below the knee, tops the list of Winter Olympic Paralympic medalists with a total of 27 medals, 22 of which are gold, in Nordic skiing.
- **Li Duan** of China was born blind. Since 2000, he has been competing in track and field events and has won four gold, two silver, and two bronze medals. At the 2008 Paralympic Games in Beijing, he broke the world record in Triple Jump. At the 2012 Games in London, he won a bronze model in Long Jump and a silver in Triple Jump.
- Despite being born with a severe spinal disability called myelodysplasia, track athlete **Louise Sauvage** of Australia went on to become a double gold and single silver medalist and a national star at the 2000 Summer Paralympic Games in Sydney.

8   A 2010 study conducted at the University of British Columbia showed that the Paralympic Games in Vancouver had a direct impact on companies' willingness to hire people with disabilities, as well as on wheelchair accessibility to buildings and public places. In the end, the Paralympics are not just about winners finding their place on the podium, but about all disabled people receiving equal status in society.

Vocabulary

Organizing vocabulary *List the nouns from the reading text that relate to the following headings. An example has been provided for each heading.*

Disabilities

paraplegic

_____

_____

_____

_____

_____

_____

_____

_____

_____

_____

Sports events

archery

_____

_____

_____

_____

_____

_____

_____

_____

_____

_____

_____

_____

_____

_____

_____

_____

Understanding vocabulary *Match each word in column 1 with its definition in column 2. Then, indicate each word's part of speech (n., v., or adj.).*

_____ 1. expand _____
_____ 2. accommodate _____
_____ 3. advocate _____
_____ 4. classify _____
_____ 5. competition _____
_____ 6. dominate _____
_____ 7. elite _____
_____ 8. evaluation _____
_____ 9. enrich _____
_____ 10. impairment _____
_____ 11. participate _____
_____ 12. modify _____
_____ 13. require _____
_____ 14. rehabilitate _____
_____ 15. therapy _____

a. the state of having a disability
b. put in a particular group or category
c. prepare for a normal life by means of therapy
d. make or become larger
e. the best in a society or organization
f. make partial changes to
g. an event or contest
h. improve the quality or value of
i. adapt to or fit in with
j. treatment to heal a medical condition
k. be the most important or noticeable thing
l. an assessment of value
m. take part in an activity or event
n. publicly support or speak on behalf of
o. need something for a purpose

EXERCISE 14·3

Using vocabulary *For each of the following items, two words from the same root are listed. Complete each sentence with the correct words. Be sure to use the correct form of each verb and to pluralize nouns, if necessary.*

1. expand, expansion

   The new electronics store is so successful that it is going to _____ and move to a bigger building.

   The store's _____ will bring in more customers.

2. accommodate, accommodation

   The Olympic Village provides _____ for competing athletes.

   Public buildings should be constructed to _____ people in wheelchairs.

3. advocate, advocacy

   The group's trip to the Amazon resulted in their _____ of rainforest protection and conservation.

   The Green Party _____ the use of renewable energy.

4. classify, classification

   Library books are _____ according to their subject matter.

   Library books are often arranged according to the Dewey Decimal _____ system.

5. compete, competition

   In 2010, more than 45,000 runners _____ in the New York Marathon.

   The _____ is open to participants from all over the world.

6. dominate, domination

   The opposing team skated hard, but there was nothing they could do to end the Rangers'

   _____ of the game.

   The Rangers _____ the ice for most of the hockey game.

7. elite, elitist

   Only _____ athletes are chosen to represent their country in the Olympics.

   Some critics accuse the Olympics of being an _____ event.

8. evaluate, evaluation

   I hope you will agree with my _____ of the situation.

   Before you can make a decision, you have to _____ your choices.

9. enrich, enrichment

The time I spent living in a foreign country certainly contributed to my cultural
_____.

Watching movies and videos can _____ your vocabulary.

10. impair, impairment

Alcohol definitely _____ your ability to react; therefore you shouldn't
drink and drive.

Drinking alcohol definitely causes an _____ of one's ability to react
quickly to dangerous situations.

11. participate, participation

Every year, thousands of school children _____ in the Terry Fox Run.

_____ in the Terry Fox Run is increasing from year to year.

12. modify, modification

When we looked at the plans for our new house, we asked the architect to make a few
_____.

The architect agreed to _____ the house plans as we requested.

13. require, requirement

The university _____ first-year students to take an English course.

An English course is a _____ for first-year students.

14. rehabilitate, rehabilitation

When the patient was released from the clinic, he had to attend a _____
program for recovering drug addicts.

The program is designed to _____ recovering drug addicts.

15. therapy, therapeutic

Massage _____ is very good for stiff or sore muscles.

The massage treatment was very _____.

Reading comprehension

Reading for main ideas *Choose the most appropriate answer to complete each of the following sentences.*

1. The Paralympics are an international sports event for _____.
   a. athletes with intellectual disabilities only
   b. athletes with physical disabilities only
   c. athletes with primarily physical disabilities, but also those with intellectual disabilities

2. The Paralympics were founded _____.
   a. to rehabilitate ex-soldiers with war injuries
   b. to develop disabled athletes' sense of self-worth
   c. to raise money for research into disabilities

3. The Paralympics are held _____.
   a. every four years before the Olympic Games
   b. every four years following the Olympic Games
   c. every four years at the same time as the Olympic Games

4. Over the years, the Paralympics have _____.
   a. grown tremendously
   b. grown moderately
   c. hardly grown at all

5. Athletes competing in the Paralympics are classified according to _____.
   a. type of disability
   b. the reason for their disability
   c. level of disability

6. Sports events at the Paralympics _____.
   a. are the same as at the Olympics
   b. are less challenging than at the Olympics
   c. have been modified or created for the Paralympics

7. Financial support from government and media recognition for the Paralympics are _____.
   a. less than for the Olympics
   b. the same as for the Olympics
   c. greater than for the Olympics

8. A study conducted by the University of British Columbia showed that the Paralympics had a positive impact on _____.
   a. employment opportunities for disabled people
   b. wheelchair accessibility in public places
   c. both

Reading for details *Rewrite the following sentences, correcting the errors.*
Some statements may have more than one error.

1. The first official competition for athletes with disabilities was held in 1896 in Rome, Italy.

   _____

2. Dr. Ludwig Grossman, the "father of sports," organized the International Stoke Mandeville
   Games in Holland.

   _____

3. The first officially recognized Paralympic Games were held in 1952 in London, England.

   _____

4. The first Paralympic Winter Games took place in Norway in 1992.

   _____

5. The Paralympics are overseen by the International Olympic Committee in Lausanne,
   Switzerland.

   _____

6. Paralympic athletes are classified according to their physical and intellectual disabilities,
   and these are broken down into four categories: amputees, those with cerebral palsy,
   those with spinal cord injuries, and those with intellectual impairment.

   _____

7. Athletes are evaluated by general practitioners.

   _____

8. There are 20 sports in the winter games and 5 in the summer games.

   _____

9. In the biathlon event, skis are specially modified for visually impaired participants.

   _____

10. Football-7-a-side was designed for wheelchair athletes, and goalball for athletes with
    intellectual impairments.

    _____

EXERCISE
14·6

Reading for facts and figures *Complete the following sentences with details from the reading text.*

1. The first disabled athletes competed in the event of _____.

2. The Paralympics have shared venues with the Olympic Games since the

   _____ Winter Games in _____ and the

   _____ Summer Games in _____.

3. Ragnhild Myklebust has won a total of _____ gold medals in

   _____.

4. _____ holds the record as the most successful Paralympic athlete.

5. Ice sledge hockey was invented in _____ and is open to athletes with

   _____.

6. Goalball is played by teams of _____ with a ball containing

   _____.

7. Skiers with disabilities affecting their legs use a _____.

8. Li Duan competes in _____ events.

9. In the 2008 Summer Paralympic Games in _____, _____

   Paralympic athletes from _____ countries competed.

10. Louise Sauvage became a national star at the _____ Paralympics

    in _____.

The Paralympics: Believe in yourself   **167**

Reading for meaning *For each of the following statements quoted from the reading text, choose the answer that is implied by the statement.*

1. "After the joy and drama surrounding record setters and record breakers, the closing ceremony of the Olympics seems anticlimactic—unless we look beyond and into the shadows where athletes show what they are really made of during the world's second biggest international elite sporting event, the Paralympics."
   a. The Paralympics get the same amount of attention as the Olympics.
   b. The Paralympics get more attention than the Olympics.
   c. The Paralympics get less attention than the Olympics.

2. "Since September 22, 1989, the Paralympics have been overseen by the International Paralympic Committee (IPC), an international nonprofit organization with headquarters in Düsseldorf, Germany."
   a. The Paralympics have an organizational structure similar to that of the Olympics.
   b. The Paralympics have an organizational structure different from that of the Olympics.

3. "To qualify for competition, athletes must also take part in world championships and achieve set time limits for performance."
   a. Paralympic athletes have to meet standards similar to those of Olympic athletes.
   b. Paralympic athletes have to meet standards different from those of Olympic athletes.

4. "Some traditional sports events have been modified to accommodate various disabilities and impairments, while others have been specially created."
   a. Paralympic events are the same as Olympic events.
   b. Paralympic events are somewhat different from Olympic events.
   c. Paralympic events are completely different from Olympic events.

5. "Paralympic medalists are not as heavily supported by their governments—or as publicly celebrated—as their Olympic counterparts. The following incomplete list confirms how deserving Paralympians are of admiration and recognition."
   a. Paralympic and Olympic athletes receive equal acknowledgment and support.
   b. Paralympic athletes do not receive any acknowledgment or support.
   c. Paralympic athletes should receive more acknowledgment and support.

Reading skills

EXERCISE
14·8

Outline *Fill in the outline below with the most important details from the reading text.*

History of the Paralympics

    Founder _____

    His reason _____

    First competition for adults with disabilities _____

    1952 _____

    1960 _____

    1976 _____

    2008 _____

Disabilities and impairments _____

_____

Paralympic events _____

_____

Paralympic heroes _____

_____

Positive impact _____

_____

_____

_____

Web search and writing

The activities on the next two pages prompt you to share information with a study partner and to search the Web for more information about famous people with disabilities.

Overcoming disabilities

"You'll never know what you can do or achieve until you try."—Louise Sauvage

ACTIVITY 14·1

Exchange experiences *Ask your partner the following questions, and add a question of your own.*

1. Do you know anyone who has a physical disability? What does the person do to overcome his or her disability?

   _____

2. Which of the following people have you heard of?

   ☐ Christy Brown   ☐ Helen Keller
   ☐ Michael J. Fox   ☐ Marlee Matlin
   ☐ Temple Grandin   ☐ Christopher Reeve
   ☐ Rick Hansen   ☐ Vincent van Gogh
   ☐ Stephen Hawking   ☐ Nick Vujicic
   ☐ Frida Kahlo   ☐ Stevie Wonder

   What disabilities or illness did/do these people have and what were they / have they been able to achieve?

   _____
   _____
   _____
   _____
   _____
   _____
   _____
   _____
   _____
   _____
   _____
   _____

3. Your question _____

Discussion *Share your answers with another partner or with the whole group.*

ACTIVITY 14·2

Web search *Find information about three of the famous disabled people listed in Question 2 of Activity 14-1, or about any other famous disabled person that you know of.*

Name of person   _____

URL   www._____

His or her disability   _____

His or her achievements   _____

    _____

Name of person   _____

URL   www._____

His or her disability   _____

His or her achievements   _____

    _____

Name of person   _____

URL   www._____

His or her disability   _____

His or her achievements   _____

    _____

ACTIVITY 14·3

Writing *Choose one of the three disabled people listed in Activity 14-2, and write a list of questions you would like to ask if you had the chance to interview him or her.*

Superman
Everyone's superhero

Pre-reading

In your culture, are there any stories of beings with superhuman powers?

_____

What special powers or qualities do they have? Do they use their special powers for good or evil purposes?

_____

Who is your favorite superhero? _____

Reading text

1   "Faster than a speeding bullet! More powerful than a locomotive! Able to leap tall buildings in a single bound! Look! Up in the sky! It's a bird! It's a plane! It's Superman!"

2   Those famous words opened the radio show _The Adventures of Superman_ in February 1940, announcing the arrival of American icon and international superhero Superman. It was not in radio, however, but in comic books that the Man of Steel made his name. Without Superman, comic books would not have rooted themselves in American culture, nor would they have spawned the awe-inspiring league of Batman, the Flash, the Green Lantern, Superboy, and Supergirl, and captured the imagination of children and adults alike for nearly three quarters of a century.

The creation of Superman

3   Superman was created in 1938 by Jerry Siegel and Joe Shuster, who went to high school together in Cleveland, Ohio. Science fiction fans who would probably be considered "nerds" today, Siegel and Shuster grew up in the Depression, when science fiction and pulp fiction magazines with titles like _Amazing Stories_ and _Weird Tales_ offered an escape for kids from poor working-class backgrounds. Joe was a budding artist and Jerry an aspiring writer, and together they dreamed of their own nationally syndicated comic strip[1] featuring a heroic, charismatic fig-

---

[1] At the time, comic strips were appearing regularly in newspapers, and the Sunday edition featured a full-page supplement of America's favorite comic strips. The supplement came to be known as the "funny papers" or "funnies." Reading the funnies was a Sunday morning ritual in many North American households.

ure like the swashbuckling actor Douglas Fairbanks, or fictional strongmen Tarzan and Buck Rogers.

4   In 1932, Siegel and Shuster put out their own magazine, *Science Fiction: The Advance Guard of Future Civilization*. In Siegel's story, "The Reign of the Superman," a homeless man, turned into a monster by a mad professor, uses his mental powers to **accumulate** great wealth through dishonest means. *Science Fiction* lasted only five issues, but the ambitious duo was determined to make it into national print. At the time, collections of newspaper comic strips reprinted in booklet form were selling with great success. When Siegel and Shuster discovered that Consolidated Book Publishers had released a black-and-white comic book with original material called *Detective Dan: Secret Operative* No. 48, they submitted "The Superman." The publisher sent them an encouraging response, but quit the comic business before a second edition could materialize.

5   Shuster burned the manuscript, but Siegel worked on a new version of Superman. This time, their hero was a good guy and savior in the tradition of Moses, Samson, and Hercules, and he used his superpowers to fight for truth, justice, and the American way of life. He wore a bright blue costume with a red cape and a diamond-shaped *S* emblazoned on his chest. Superman's birth father, Jor-El, had sent his infant son, Kal-El, from the doomed planet of Krypton to the safety of Earth in a rocket, and he was raised in an orphanage. Later, the story would be changed, and Superman would be raised by a kind elderly couple, Jonathan and Martha Kent, from Smallville, Kansas. Unaware of his powers until the age of 18, when his adoptive parents explained how they had found him in a field, the boy grew up as Clark Kent and became a newspaper reporter for the *Daily Planet*. Superman's alter ego, Clark Kent, was myopic, socially awkward, and meek, but he was also intelligent, hard-working, and decent to the core—the kind of guy no one, including his pretty, feisty, and disdainful co-reporter, Lois Lane, would ever **suspect** of having superhuman powers.

6   Despite Superman's makeover, newspaper syndicates weren't interested in the story. After five years of rejections and false leads, Siegel and Shuster finally got an offer in 1938 from Detective Comics, Inc. (later to become DC Comics) to produce 13 pages of *Superman*. Without any previous publicity, *Action Comics* No. 1 became an instant success. Sales **approached** half a million copies after 11 issues, and soon doubled. In subsequent issues, the stories focused on contemporary issues of unjust imprisonment, domestic abuse, corruption, labor problems, and disarmament. With the Great Depression not yet over and war looming in Europe, the time was right for a larger-than-life hero who came to the aid of ordinary people in **distress**.

7   After having been rejected by every newspaper syndicate in the United States, *Superman* finally came out in January 1939 as a black-and-white newspaper strip, and in November of that year as a color page in the Sunday newspaper. The strip ran until 1966, and again from 1977 to 1983, making *Superman* the most successful adventure comic strip ever. In the summer of 1939, one year after appearing in *Action Comics*, Superman got his own comic book, and until 1988 he appeared on every cover. Altogether, the king of comics headlined *Superman*, *Action Comics*, and *The World's Finest Comics*, with guest appearances in *All Star Comics* alongside a group of popular superheroes known as the Justice Society of America. From then on, Superman never looked back.

Superman's career

8   The Golden Age (1938–1956) established the character of Superman, his world, and his place in the booming comic book business. In addition to the ability to fly, Superman's powers included X-ray, telescopic, and microscopic vision, and these powers were added to over time. Although **exposure** to the element kryptonite could mean his downfall, he was invulnerable to fallout from atomic bombs. The Ultra-Humanite, the Archer, the Puzzler, the Prankster, the Toyman, Mr. Mxyztplk, J. Wilbur Wolfingham, Bizarro, and Brainiac were introduced as formidable foes, but his archenemy Lex Luthor continued to **torment** the Man of Steel throughout his career. Natu-

rally, Superman's popularity gave rise to other superheroes, and Superman regularly teamed up with fellow crime fighters Batman and Robin in *The World's Finest Comics* until 1986.

9   The story of Superman would not be complete without office boy Jimmy Olsen or girl reporter Lois Lane, both of whom were **spun off** into their own successful comic books. Other memorable secondary characters appeared along the way, but Jimmy Olsen and Lois Lane remained the most significant. In 1945, Superboy came on the scene, and in 1949, *The Adventures of Superman When He Was a Boy* went on to become its own series. In 1955, Superboy was reunited with his pets, Krypto the Superdog and Beppo the Supermonkey. In 1959, Kara Zor-El, or Supergirl, made her debut and was joined by Streaky the Supercat and Comet the Super-Horse.

10   At first, Siegel and Shuster were involved in the production of Superman, but as the comic book's popularity grew, more artists were brought in, and eventually Siegel and Shuster lost control of their creation. They had already given up ownership of Superman when they sold the rights to National Comics for $130. In 1947, Siegel and Shuster **sued** DC Comics for $5 million, but they lost their **claim** and settled for $100,000, something they would bitterly regret. When talk of a big-budget movie circulated in the mid-1970s, Siegel and Shuster made their case for **compensation** known to the press, which resulted in Warner Brothers giving them pensions and **reinstating** them as the official creators of Superman.[2]

11   Throughout his long career, Superman has undergone numerous transformations as he moved through the differing eras and styles of comic books—the Silver Age (1957–1969), the Bronze Age (1970–1985), and the Steel Age (1986–present). Various artists have made the original Man of Steel bigger and stronger, and given him a hunkier, more chiseled and glamorous look. As early as 1941, his social **conscience diminished**, and his **exploits** focused on fighting crime syndicates, evil megalomaniacs, and alien forces with superpowers of their own. Over his career Superman has fought battles on Earth, on Earth-2, and in space. He has split into two—Superman Red and Superman Blue—and returned as his old self. Once, he even died, but came back to life shortly after. With the rocky relationship of the past behind them, Lois Lane and Clark Kent married, and he did the unthinkable by revealing to her the identity he'd kept secret since the beginning. Superman's stories and his history have been told in best-selling miniseries, and although Superman has come to define American comic books, he has also starred in radio, television, animated films, and motion pictures.

12   Of his many **accomplishments**, the most amazing is undoubtedly Superman's appeal to each new generation. By keeping up with the times, Superman has achieved the impossible: Superman will never die.

Superman's milestones[3]

1938   Superman debuts in *Action Comics*.

1939   *Superman* newspaper comic strip is nationally syndicated.

           Action Comics gives Superman his own comic.

           Superman toys are manufactured, and Superman's face appears on numerous products.

1940   The radio show *The Adventures of Superman* premieres.

           Among Superman products are puzzles, paint sets, paper dolls, games, greeting cards, coloring books, candy, bubble gum, wood and metal figures, Superman Krypto-Raygun, and clothes.

---

[2] In 1975, DC Comics honored Siegel and Shuster in an issue where Superman meets Joseph J. Jerome, a castaway who believes himself to be Superman's creator. A second tribute was presented in 1984, when two boys named Jerry and Joe reinvent Superman after invading aliens wipe out all earthly heroes.

[3] Adapted from Scott Beatty's *Superman: The Ultimate Guide to the Man of Steel* (New York: DC Comics, 2006).

1941   Superman appears in *The World's Finest Comics*, along with Batman and Robin.

An animated cartoon series runs in theaters until 1943; a short film receives an Academy Award nomination.

1942   The 15-minute radio show is picked up by Mutual Network and runs every Monday, Wednesday, and Friday.

1948   The movie serial *Superman*, produced by Columbia, becomes the most financially successful serial despite cost-cutting production and crude animation effects. It is followed in 1950 by a 15-part series, *Atom Man vs. Superman*.

1953   *The Adventures of Superman* television series begins on Saturday matinee. Over the next 40 years, 104 episodes run.

1962   *Superman* reaches its 150th issue.

1966   A Broadway musical, *It's a Bird, It's a Plane, It's Superman*, opens in March, but closes after 128 performances.

1978   Superman hits movie theaters with *Superman: The Movie*, starring Christopher Reeve and Margot Kidder. This is followed by *Superman II* (1980), *Superman III* (1983), and *Superman IV: The Quest for Peace* (1987).

Superman and *Action Comics* celebrate 40 years together.

1984   DC Comics pays tribute to Siegel and Shuster in an issue where two young boys, named Jerry and Joe, re-create Superman after the Earth is invaded by aliens.

1992   Superman is killed in a battle with Doomsday in *Superman* No. 75, but returns to life in September in *Action Comics* No. 689. *The Death of Superman* sells six million copies.

1993   The television series *Lois and Clark: The New Adventures of Superman* begins; it runs until 1997.

1996   Clark Kent and Lois Lane get married in *Superman: The Wedding Album*.

1997   Superman gets a new look with a new costume, plus energy-based powers.

1998   Superman celebrates his 60th anniversary, and goes back to his old costume and powers.

1999   *Superman* celebrates its 750th issue, and DC Comics celebrates its history as one of the longest-running comic book series in America.

2001   The television series *Smallville*, about the early life of Clark Kent, debuts; it runs until 2010.

2003   DC Comics looks at Superman's impact in a special 800th-anniversary issue.

2005   A seven-issue *Infinite Crisis* is launched for a new generation.

2006   Warner Brother releases *Superman Returns*, with Superman returning to Earth after a five-year absence.

2013   *Superman: Man of Steel* is scheduled to appear in movie theaters.

Vocabulary

EXERCISE
15·1

Organizing vocabulary *List the nouns and adjectives in the reading text that describe superheroes.*

Nouns (4) _savior,_ _____

Adjectives (6) _heroic,_ _____

_____

EXERCISE
15·2

Understanding vocabulary *Complete the following chart with the correct form of each of the words and phrases from the reading text. Then, using a dictionary, indicate the definition of each word or phrase.*

Noun	Adjective	Verb	Definition
1. accomplishment	_____	_____	_____
2. claim	X	_____	_____
3. compensation	_____	_____	_____
4. distress	_____	_____	_____
5. exposure	_____	_____	_____
6. exploit	_____	_____	_____
7. _____	_____	accumulate	_____
8. _____	_____	approach	_____
9. _____	diminished	_____	_____
10. _____	X	reinstate	_____
11. _____	X	spin off	_____
12. _____	_____	suspect	_____
13. conscience	_____	X	_____
14. _____	X	sue	_____
15. _____	X	torment	_____

Using vocabulary *Answer each of the following questions, using the underlined word or phrase in your answer.*

1. What is one of mankind's greatest scientific <u>accomplishments</u>?

   _____

2. How many points can you <u>accumulate</u> when you play your favorite video or computer game?

   _____

3. How can you tell when bad weather is <u>approaching</u>?

   _____

4. If you have travel insurance, what <u>claims</u> can you submit to the insurance company?

   _____

5. When people are injured in an accident, what kind of <u>compensation</u> can they receive?

   _____

6. How do you feel when your <u>conscience</u> bothers you?

   _____

7. Why is the population of some wild animals <u>diminishing</u>?

   _____

8. What is the international <u>distress</u> signal for people in trouble?

   _____

9. What problems can <u>exposure</u> to chemicals cause?

   _____

10. Why do people like to read about the <u>exploits</u> of explorers and adventurers?

    _____

11. If someone is fired from his job without a good reason, should the person be <u>reinstated</u>?

    _____

12. How many different products were <u>spun off</u> from the *Harry Potter* series?

    _____

13. If one person wants to <u>sue</u> another person, whose help does he need?

    _____

14. If your cell phone were stolen, whom would you <u>suspect</u>?

    _____

15. Why do bullies like to <u>torment</u> other students?

    _____

Reading comprehension

Reading for main ideas *Choose the boldface word or phrase that correctly completes each of the following statements.*

1. The appearance of Superman **changed** | **didn't change** the course of comic book history.

2. Superman **has become** | **hasn't become** an American icon.

3. Superman **is** | **isn't** the most popular and well-known comic book figure of all time.

4. Superman's creators **gave up early** | **never gave up** on their idea of a syndicated comic strip.

5. Superman's appearance and powers **have stayed** | **haven't stayed** the same throughout history.

6. Throughout his career, Superman **has represented** | **hasn't represented** the fight for truth, justice, and the American way of life.

7. Superman **is** | **isn't** the most successful adventure comic strip ever.

Reading for details *Answer each of the following questions with information from the reading text.*

1. Who created Superman?

_____

2. Who is Clark Kent? What is his job?

_____

3. What other name is Superman known by?

_____

4. Who made the first offer to publish *Superman*, and in what year?

_____

5. Why did Superman become an instant success?

_____

6. What other superheroes came after Superman?

_____

7. Which comic books have featured Superman?

_____

8. How have Superman's transformations been classified?

_____

9. Where has Superman appeared besides in comic books?

_____

10. Where do the words "It's a bird! It's a plane! It's Superman!" come from?

_____

EXERCISE
15·6

Reading for facts and figures *Indicate the year in which each of the following events in Superman's history occurred.*

1. _____ *Lois and Clark: The New Adventures of Superman* debuts on television.

2. _____ *Superman Returns* is released by Warner Brothers.

3. _____ The radio show *The Adventures of Superman* premieres.

4. _____ The television show *The Adventures of Superman* premieres.

5. _____ Superman celebrates his 60th anniversary.

6. _____ *Superman: The Movie* opens in movie theaters.

7. _____ Superman dies in battle, but comes back to life.

8. _____ The first issue of *Superman* is published.

9. _____ The 150th issue of *Superman* is published.

10. _____ The 750th issue of *Superman* is published.

Reading for meaning *Using the information in the statement from the reading text, answer each of the following questions.*

1. "Without Superman, comic books would not have rooted themselves in American culture." Would comic books have become so popular if Superman hadn't been invented?
   ☐ Yes
   ☐ No

2. "*Science Fiction* lasted only five issues, but the ambitious duo was determined to make it into national print." Did Siegel and Shuster believe that *Superman* would ever be published?
   ☐ Yes
   ☐ No

3. "With the Great Depression not yet over and war looming in Europe, the time was right for a larger-than-life hero who came to the aid of ordinary people in distress." Were the late 1930s a bad time for a story like *Superman*?
   ☐ Yes
   ☐ No

4. "Altogether, the king of comics headlined *Superman, Action Comics,* and *The World's Finest Comics,* with guest appearances in *All Star Comics* alongside a group of popular superheroes known as the Justice Society of America. From then on, Superman never looked back." Did Superman become even less successful after his appearance in *All Star Comics*?
   ☐ Yes
   ☐ No

5. "At first, Siegel and Shuster were involved in the production of Superman, but as the comic book's popularity grew, more artists were brought in, and eventually Siegel and Shuster lost control of their creation." As Superman's popularity grew, did Siegel and Shuster continue to play an important creative role?
   ☐ Yes
   ☐ No

Reading skills

Biography *Complete Superman's biography with details from the reading text.*

Birth name _____

Place of birth _____

Birth father _____

Human name _____

Adoptive parents _____

Hometown _____

Wife's name _____

Job _____

Personality of Clark Kent _____

Superpowers _____

_____

Weakness _____

Costume _____

Colleagues _____

Friends _____

Enemies _____

_____

Mission _____

Feats and accomplishments _____

_____

Web search and writing

The activities on the next two pages prompt you to share information with a study partner and to search the Web for more information about amazing superheroes, and record the information below.

Amazing superheroes

ACTIVITY 15·1

Exchange experiences *Ask your partner the following questions, and add a question of your own.*

1. Which of the following superheroes are you familiar with?

☐ Batman
☐ Captain America
☐ The Green Lantern
☐ The Incredible Hulk
☐ Iron Man

☐ The Punisher
☐ Spider-Man
☐ Thor
☐ Wolverine
☐ Wonder Woman

2. What special powers does a superhero possess?

_____

3. Your question _____

Discussion *Share your answers with another partner or with the whole group.*

_____

ACTIVITY 15·2

Search the Web *Find information about amazing superheroes that you admire, and record the following details.*

Name of superhero   _____

URL   www._____

Abilities and powers   _____

_____

_____

Name of superhero _____

URL www._____

Abilities and powers _____

_____

_____

Name of superhero _____

URL www._____

Abilities and powers _____

_____

_____

ACTIVITY
15·3

Writing *Create your own superhero, and write a profile that includes his or her name, alter ego, origins, special powers and abilities, physical description, and costume.*

Answer key

1 Bananas about bananas

1·1 Diseases and ailments (all n.): high blood pressure, irritation, diarrhea, stroke, wound, ulcer, rash, heartburn, cancer, osteoporosis, anemia, stress

Parts of the body (all n.): heart, stomach, immune system, kidney, cartilage, brain, bowels, bone

Substances with a healthful effect (all n.): antioxidant, calcium, antifungal [agent], antacid, fatty acids, serotonin, anti-inflammatory, antibiotic [agent]

Medical treatments (all v.): prevent, cure, detoxify, restore, soothe, relieve, heal

1·2
1. packed with (adj.)
2. consume (v.)
3. boosted (v.)
4. cultivated (v.)
5. ripen (v.)
6. originated in (v.)
7. bunch (n.)
8. nutrients (n.)
9. ensure (v.)
10. propagated (v.)
11. sustain (v.)
12. commodities (n.)
13. commercialization (n.)
14. versatility (n.)
15. output (n.)

1·3
1. T
2. F
3. T
4. T
5. F
6. T
7. T
8. F
9. T
10. F

1·4
1. b
2. c
3. a
4. b
5. a
6. b
7. a
8. c
9. a
10. b

1·5
1. 9 inches
2. 75 percent
3. 10–20
4. 20–45 kilos
5. 110–140
6. Division
7. .6 meter wide, 2.75 meters long
8. 6–7.6 meters
9. Ample water, rich soil, and good drainage
10. Mexico, Costa Rica, Brazil, Colombia, Ecuador, the Philippines
11. 1,200

1·6
1. Agree, Paragraph 1
2. Disagree, Paragraph 12
3. Agree, Paragraph 8
4. Agree, Paragraph 8
5. Neither, —

1·7
Heart and blood production
1. Reduce risk of high blood pressure and stroke
2. Regulate heartbeat
3. Ensure production of hemoglobin
4. Prevent anemia
Mental health and brain function
1. Relieve stress (via potassium)
2. Increase the ability to learn
Bone building
1. Allow absorption of calcium
2. Help lubricate cartilage (via manganese)
Kidney protection
1. Detoxify the kidneys
2. Lower the risk of kidney cancer in women
Digestion
1. Reduce acidity and irritation in the stomach lining
2. Keep digested food moving through the bowels
3. Restore electrolytes
Skin
1. Soothe insect bites
2. Relieve rashes and skin irritations
3. Heal wounds
4. Help remove warts
Other
1. Cure or relieve morning sickness and hangovers
2. Can improve eyesight
3. Help a person quit smoking

2   Schloss Neuschwanstein: A king and his castle

2·1
1. take the throne, reign, royal status, coronation, depose, Duchess, Empress, monarch, king
2. mystique, enigma, speculation, suspicious circumstances
3. eccentric, mad, insane, mentally ill
4. saga, legend, theme, fairy tale
5. frescoes, poetry, theater, composer, opera, musical capital
6. construction, complete, model, plan, design, commission
7. gothic, baroque, rococo, neoromantic, neo-French
8. lavish, ornate, luxury, elaborate, opulent

2·2
1. indulgence, indulgent
2. reign, reigning
3. aloof
4. commission
5. crown
6. deposition
7. eccentricity
8. enigmatic
9. inherit
10. holiness
11. interment
12. opulence
13. —
14. —
15. mystical

2·3
1. holy
2. mystique
3. commissioned
4. amenities
5. reigned
6. interred
7. eccentric
8. indulge
9. opulent
10. deposed
11. heirs
12. aloofness
13. coronation
14. enigmas
15. legacy

2·4
Paragraph 1: f
Paragraph 2: i
Paragraph 3: a
Paragraph 4: e
Paragraph 5: h
Paragraph 6: d
Paragraph 7: b
Paragraph 8: g
Paragraph 9: c

2·5
1. art, music, poetry, and theater
2. He believed in a holy kingdom and wanted to make his fantasies a reality.
3. as a personal retreat in the mountains
4. a central heating system, running cold and hot water, flush toilets, an electric intercom system, a telephone, and a dumbwaiter to transport food from the kitchen to the dining room
5. He used his personal fortune, and when that ran out, he borrowed heavily from foreign banks.
6. because of his eccentric behavior
7. He slept during the day and was active at night; he dressed in historical costumes; he traveled in elaborate coaches and sleighs; he withdrew from public life; and he never married.
8. He drowned in Lake Starnberg under suspicious circumstances.

2·6

1. 1.3 million
2. Sleeping Beauty's
3. Richard Wagner
4. 15
5. southern
6. 12 euros
7. neoromantic
8. 18
9. Munich
10. royal palace of Herrenchiemsee

2·7   *Suggested answers:*

1. had; Paragraph 3 (He was tall, slim, handsome, and a king.)
2. didn't want; Paragraph 3 (He tended to spend more time alone indulging his fantasies than training to become a future king.)
3. was; Paragraph 8 (Ludwig was known to be a strong swimmer and no water was found in his lungs. No investigation was ever made into the suspicious circumstances surrounding his death.)
4. was; Paragraph 7 (He withdrew from public life, shirked his duties, and engaged in increasingly eccentric behavior that earned him the nickname "Mad King Ludwig." In 1875, he began sleeping during the day and being active at night. He traveled in elaborate coaches and sleighs, and he dressed in historical costumes.)
   OR wasn't; Paragraph 8 (Dr. Bernhard von Gudden certified Ludwig as mentally ill without a psychiatric examination.)
5. didn't entertain; Paragraph 5 (Ludwig built beautiful and costly castles, which strangers were not allowed to enter.)
6. wasn't; Paragraph 7 (When Ludwig's personal finances ran dry, he borrowed heavily from foreign banks. Despite his mounting debt and the advice of his financial ministers, Ludwig took on more opulent projects.)
7. wasn't; Paragraph 8 (On June 10, 1886, a government commission declared Ludwig insane, and he was deposed, taken into custody, and transported to Castle Berg on Lake Starnberg.)
8. hated; Paragraph 7 (He withdrew from public life, shirked his duties, and engaged in increasingly eccentric behavior that earned him the nickname "Mad King Ludwig.")
9. wasn't; Paragraph 4 (Ludwig's lack of political experience and his shy nature made him ill-suited to the throne of Bavaria. In 1866, two years after his coronation, Ludwig experienced a humiliating defeat when he was forced into an alliance with Prussia against Austria.)
10. is; Paragraph 9 (He has become an idealized and tragic figure, much like a character in a gothic romance novel, and the subject of biographies and movies.)

2·8

1845: Ludwig is born on August 25.
1864: King Maximilian dies suddenly and Ludwig II takes the throne at the age of 18.
1866: Ludwig suffers a personal defeat when he is forced into an alliance with Prussia.
1867: Ludwig becomes engaged to Duchess Sophie Charlotte in Bavaria, but breaks it off.
   He commissions the building of Schloss Neuschwanstein.
1869: Construction of Schloss Neuschwanstein begins.
1874: Construction of Schloss Linderhof begins.
1875: Ludwig withdraws from public life, and his behavior becomes increasingly eccentric.
1878: Construction of the royal palace of Herrenchiemsee begins.
1884: Ludwig moves into his private suite in Schloss Neuschwanstein.
1886: On June 10, Ludwig is declared insane and deposed.
   On June 12, he is arrested and taken to Castle Berg.
   On June 13, he drowns in Lake Starnberg and is interred on June 19.

3 The Three Racketeers: Wildlife experiences on a small island

3·1
1. scurry, climb, saunter, scoot, topple, slide, skitter, race
2. scuffle, combat, skirmish
3. attack, squabble, tussle
4. forage, munch, feed, chew, swallow
5. growl, yelp, warble, coo, whistle
6. show up, come around, turn up, appear
7. upstage, garden stage, parade, showtime
8. rustic, wooded, parklike, woods, deer trails, rocky terraces
9. get a look at, spot, gaze at
10. crew, huddle, trio, family, bunch

3-2
1. h
2. d
3. e
4. l
5. m
6. b
7. n
8. i
9. k
10. o
11. g
12. a
13. j
14. c
15. f

3·3
1. inevitable
2. alert
3. terminate
4. agile
5. blends
6. rustic
7. vigilant
8. resumed
9. sporadic
10. irresistible
11. huddle
12. sturdy
13. attitude
14. check out
15. tactics

3·4
1. The Hartleys moved to Mayne Island to live a quiet, simple life and be close to nature.
2. They welcomed all animals that appeared on their property. They let all the animals, including insects, make themselves at home.
3. They were curious and excited, and couldn't wait for him to reappear.
4. They didn't get along, with each trying to get the most food.
5. They called their property the "garden stage," because it became a kind of theater where the raccoons performed and entertained.
6. Their most entertaining experience occurred when the two female raccoons brought their young.
7. They enjoyed watching the young raccoons learn to climb up and down trees.

3·5
    1. F
    2. T
    3. F
    4. T
    5. T
    6. F
    7. T
    8. F
    9. T
    10. T

3·6
Suggested answers:
raccoons have a bushy ringed tail?
raccoons have a black mask across their face and shiny black eyes?
raccoons have silver-gloved hands with five slim, agile fingers?
raccoons can pick things up with their fingers and hold them in their hands?
raccoons mate in February and litters are born in the late spring?
raccoons eat anything from bird feed to dinner leftovers to dog food?
raccoons can climb fences, sheds, and trees?
baby raccoons are very playful and like to dig in gardens?
raccoons like water?
raccoons fight with each other, but usually don't harm each other?
raccoons are very entertaining animals?
raccoons are very clever, curious, and determined?
raccoons make many kinds of noises: warbling, cooing, whistling, growling, and yelping?

3·7
    1. the hectic pace of
    2. liked
    3. legally owned
    4. were mating
    5. looked like a fighter
    6. didn't harm each other
    7. entertainers
    8. wanted to be Number One
    9. alone
    10. didn't mind

3·8
Answers will vary.

4   The lure of lost treasure ships

4·1
    1. ships, sail, armored warships, merchant vessels, freighter, submarines, cargo, maiden voyage, on board
    2. treasure, gold, silver, precious jewels, priceless antiquities, artifacts, collectibles, bounty, booty
    3. tragedy, enemy attack, natural catastrophe, peril, the bends, adverse marine and weather conditions, disaster

4·2
    1. bounty, booty
    2. locate, detect
    3. recover, salvage
    4. priceless, rewarding
    5. shipwreck, catastrophe
    6. challenge, obstacle
    7. peril, disaster
    8. artifact, collectibles
    9. lure, capture attention
    10. legendary, renowned

4·3   *Consult a dictionary for definitions.*
1. adj.
2. adj.
3. v.
4. v.
5. adj.
6. n.
7. n.
8. n.
9. v.
10. adj.
11. v.
12. adj.
13. v.
14. n.
15. n.

4·4
1. remains
2. evolved
3. doomed
4. feasible
5. laden
6. eroded
7. collided, wreck
8. subject to
9. vessels
10. miscellaneous
11. withstand
12. desecration
13. counteract
14. lure

4·5   Paragraph 1: h
Paragraph 2: c
Paragraph 3: a
Paragraph 4: i
Paragraph 5: e
Paragraph 6: b
Paragraph 7: g
Paragraph 8: d
Paragraph 9: f

4·6
1. They were carrying more than 700 tons of gold.
2. There are about three million.
3. In the past: Nets and lines were dragged across the ocean floor.
   In the present: Sonar, side-scan sonar, sub-bottom profilers, and GPS systems can detect lost ships.
4. In the past: Divers wore heavy copper and canvas equipment, could dive only to 200 feet, and suffered the bends.
   In the present: Divers use oxygen tanks and can work from submersibles for up to three days and at depths up to 20,000 feet.
5. Submersibles with robotic arms make it safer to access and investigate lost treasure ships.
6. Records of a ship's cargo may not exist; expeditions are expensive and time-consuming; there are no international agreements on who owns a ship and has the right of salvage.
7. Lost ships are gravesites and should not be disturbed.

4·7
1. a
2. d
3. f, g
4. h
5. g
6. f
7. b, e, h
8. c, d, e
9. e, g, h
10. b, c, d

4·8
1. b
2. b
3. a
4. a
5. b
6. a

4·9 Locating a lost ship
  Depth: lie thousands of meters deep in dark and dangerous waters
  Terrain: rugged and shifting
  Detection: wrecks covered in sand and mud; badly eroded materials
Accessing a lost ship
  Dangers to divers: can get the bends; accessing wrecks in deep water can be dangerous
  Time needed to investigate: can take many days when divers have to work at great depths
  Weather conditions: storms and adverse weather
Financial obstacles
  Money needed: requires large amounts of money for teams and equipment
  Value of the cargo: unknown because of absence of records
Legal and ethical issues
  Legal ownership: complex laws governing ownership of ships and their contents
  International agreements: do not exist
  Gravesites: should be preserved and not desecrated

5   Terry Fox: A real-life hero

5·1
1. diagnose, amputation, chemotherapy, treatment, artificial/prosthetic limb, hospitalize
2. cancer, osteosarcoma, bruises, blisters, shin splints, inflamed knee, cysts, dizzy spells, tendonitis, coughing, shortness of breath, disease, chest pains, pain, exhaustion
3. determination, undefeated, persistence, doggedness, tireless, undaunted, put his heart and mind to a task
4. basketball, long-distance runner, kinesiology, marathon, train, gait
5. gale-force winds, heavy rain, snowstorms, extreme heat and humidity

5·2 *Consult a dictionary for definitions.*
1. diagnosis, diagnostic
2. determinable, determine
3. inspiration, inspirational
4. persistent, persist
5. strained, strain
6. survivable, survive
7. amputee OR amputation
8. donate
9. hospital OR hospitalization
10. prosthesis
11. athlete
12. aggression
13. compassionate
14. aware
15. cancerous

5·3
1. c
2. e
3. a
4. f
5. d
6. g
7. b

5·4
1. donations
2. diagnosed, hospitalized
3. cancer
4. determination, persistence
5. athletes
6. compassion
7. inspired
8. awareness
9. strain
10. amputation, prosthetic
11. aggressive, survive

5·5
1. Terry was active in sports in high school, and he tried out for the school basketball team until he made the team.
2. Doctors told Terry that he had only a 50 percent chance of survival.
3. Terry recovered quickly from his operation because of his positive attitude and determination.
4. Terry was deeply affected by the suffering and death of other patients at the British Columbia Cancer Control Agency facility.
5. Terry decided to run a marathon across Canada because he wanted to raise money for cancer research.
6. When Terry started out, he didn't get much public support.
7. Terry had to discontinue his run because the cancer had spread to his lungs.
8. When Terry found out that the cancer had spread to his lungs, he planned to beat the disease and continue.
9. Events to raise money in Terry Fox's name take place all over the world.
10. Terry Fox is known throughout Canada and internationally.

5·6
1. right; bone; 18
2. Physical Education teacher; kinesiology
3. artificial/prosthetic limb
4. The story of an amputee who ran the New York City Marathon; marathon; $24 million; cancer research
5. the Canadian Cancer Society; corporations; the government; expenses; vehicle costs; gear; artificial limb
6. St. Johns, Newfoundland; Vancouver, British Columbia
7. 42; 5,373; Thunder Bay, Ontario; September 1, 1980
8. $1.7 million; June 28, 1981; 22
9. $600 million
10. Terry Fox Run; 1981; September

5·7
1. four
2. students who demonstrate humanitarian service as well as academic excellence
3. the Rocky Mountains
4. *Time* magazine
5. 83 kilometers
6. September 1981
7. September 18, 1980
8. two
9. March 14, 2005
10. Thunder Bay, Ottawa, St. Johns, Port Coquitlam, Victoria, Prince George, Vancouver

5·8
1. b
2. a
3. b
4. b
5. a

5·9   *Suggested characteristics:*
determination
courage
compassion
a positive attitude
dedication to a cause
an ability to inspire others
endurance

6   Storm chasers: scientists, nature freaks, or daredevils?

6·1   Natural disasters: tornado (n.), hurricane (n.), typhoon (n.), tropical cyclone (n.), drought (n.), flood (n.), torrential rain (n.), catastrophe (n.)

Weather and meteorology: thunder (n./v.), lightning (n.), rain (n./v.), hailstones (n.), condensation (n.), forecasting (n.), storm (n./v.), breeze (n.), wind (n.), ice crystals (n.), thunderstorm (n.), air (n.), atmosphere (n.), cloud (n.), moisture (n.), global warming (n.), climate change (n.)

Damage and destruction: crumpled (adj.), flattened (adj.), shattered (adj.), overturned (adj.), twisted (adj.), downed (adj.), toppled (adj.), collapsed (adj.), injure (v.), maim (v.), kill (v.), wipe (something) off the map (id.), lay waste to (id.), wreak damage (id.)

6·2
1. saturation, saturate
2. deception, deceive
3. prediction, (un)predictable
4. deployment, deployable
5. elevate, elevated
6. encirclement
7. fuel
8. forecast
9. interception
10. condense
11. track
12. exertion
13. resemblance
14. —
15. —

6·3
1. has forecast/forecasted
2. fuel
3. saturated
4. exert
5. spectacle
6. debris
7. track
8. encircled
9. resemble
10. condensation
11. deceptively
12. predict
13. intercepted
14. deployed
15. elevations

6·4
1. a
2. b
3. b
4. a
5. a

6·5   *Answers will be paraphrases of the direct quotations below.*
Paragraph 1: "Losing a loved one, or everything one owns, to a natural disaster is everyone's worst nightmare."
Paragraph 2: "Storm chasing got its start in the mid-1950s, when researchers and government employees went out into the field to gather scientific information about severe weather events."
Paragraph 3: "Although tornadoes in the United States begin with a gentle southern breeze coming off the Gulf of Mexico, the forces of nature can turn them into devils."
Paragraph 4: "Tornadoes are unpredictable in size, shape, and behavior."
Paragraph 5: "Whereas tornadoes form over land, hurricanes are born over water."
Paragraph 6: "Over the past 20 years, extreme weather has become a media spectacle."
Paragraph 7: "Storm chasing is not for the faint of heart."
Paragraph 8: "As the climate warms, convective storms will intensify, which translates into mightier Hurricane Katrinas."

6·6   1. 300 feet to 2 miles wide
         Thousands of feet high
      2. Head: shaped like a pancake, anvil, or wedge
         Tail: long, straight or bent, like a rope, drill bit, stovepipe, elephant trunk, or cone
      3. Black, white, or the color of soil
      4. A single one or several in sequence
      5. 261–381 miles per hour
      6. Early spring to fall
      7. Can turn cars into missiles and other objects into projectiles
         Injure, maim, and kill people
         Can destroy an entire town
         Cause billions of dollars in damage
      8. Moist air: moves from the Gulf of Mexico toward the Great Plains and mixes with hot, dry air from the south and cold air from the north
         The hot and cold air: force the moist air to rise
         Condensation: is sucked upward to form a huge cumulonimbus cloud
         Winds: from different directions cause the air to spin clockwise
         Moisture at the top: cools to ice crystals and forms a supercell thunderstorm
         The result: thunder, lightning, torrential rain, and hail
      9. Tornadoes form over land; hurricanes form over water.

6·7   1. August 2005; New Orleans; 1,800; $81 billion
      2. Ninety; Tornado Alley
      3. 80 million
      4. 1,690
      5. 2010; one-third; 60
      6. two to 200 miles
      7. National Severe Storms Laboratory; 1964

6·8   Do's: 1, 3, 4, 6, 7, 10, 11
      Don'ts: 2, 5, 8, 9, 12

6·9   1. People who started out as researchers and government employees
         People who like to observe and experience weather
      2. Gather scientific information
         Follow storms and record videos/photographs that they sell to television stations or post on the Internet
      3. US storm season from early spring to fall
      4. Mainly in Tornado Alley, where most storms in the US touch down
      5. In their cars and vehicles
         Laptops, cell phones, and emergency equipment
      6. To collect data about extreme weather
         For the thrill of the chase and for fame

7 Pixar Studios: Movie magic

7·1
1. feature film, motion picture, short film
2. creator, producer, director, actor, editor, animator, graphic artist
3. special effects, script, dialogue, props, set, lighting

7·2 *Consult a dictionary for definitions.*
1. n.
2. n.
3. n.
4. n.
5. n.
6. n.
7. v.
8. v.
9. n./v.
10. v.
11. v.
12. v.
13. adj.
14. adj.
15. adj.

7·3
1. approval
2. generated
3. merge
4. garnered, nominations
5. innovative
6. turnaround
7. sequels
8. manipulating
9. collaboration
10. revolutionized
11. unprecedented
12. achievement
13. pioneered
14. painstaking

7·4
1. b
2. c
3. a
4. b
5. a
6. c
7. a

7·5 6, 13, 3, 11, 14, 5, 1, 9, 4, 8, 2, 12, 7, 10

7·6
1. Pixar Studios was founded in the 1970s.
2. In 1984, Lucas recruited John Lasseter, a two-time winner of Student Film Awards while at the California Institute of the Arts, from Disney Studios.
3. Despite the graphic division's creative success, Lucas sold the group to Steve Jobs for $10 million.
4. *Tin Toy,* the first film to use this technology, won an Academy Award for Animated Short Film in 1988.
5. In May 1991, Pixar teamed up with Walt Disney Pictures to produce three animated films.
6. Hugely popular with audiences around the world, *Toy Story* became the top-grossing film of 1995, bringing in $362 million globally at box offices.
7. Together with Disney Studios Motion Pictures, Pixar Animation Studios went on to produce 10 feature films.
8. Pixar's films have earned the company 35 Academy Award nominations, nine Oscars, and six Golden Globes, plus several international awards.
9. In 2004, *Finding Nemo* took home an Oscar for Best Animated Film.
10. In 2006, Pixar merged with the Walt Disney Company.

7·7   1. Successful
          2. Unsuccessful
          3. Successful
          4. Successful
          5. Successful

7·8   1979: The Graphics Group becomes part of Lucasfilm Ltd., and uses the Pixar Image Computer to design graphics programs and to generate images and special effects.
          1984: John Lasseter joins the group.
          1986: Lucas sells the graphic division to Steve Jobs.
          1987: Pixar wins first prize in Computer-Generated Imagery at the San Francisco International Film Festival for *Luxo Jr.*, as well as its first Academy Award nomination for Best Animated Short. It invents RenderMan technology to produce graphics with photographic quality.
          1988: *Tin Toy* is the first computer-animated film to win an Academy Award.
          1995: *Toy Story* is the first feature-length computer-animated film; it is the top-grossing film of the year.
          1997: Pixar agrees to produce another five feature films for Disney.
          2004: *Finding Nemo* wins the Oscar for Best Animated Film.
          2006: Pixar merges with the Walt Disney Company.

8   Karaoke: Everyone can be a star

8·1   Musical performers (all n.): orchestra, musician, percussionist, rock band, singer, stage, Broadway
          Singing: song (n.), perform (v.), sing-along (n.), vocal cords (n.), pop (n.), country and western (n.), evergreen (n.), key (n.), vocal range (n.), lyrics (n.), larynx (n.), voice box (n.), rhythm (n.)
          Music recording: 8-track (adj.), sound track (n.), amplifier (n.), instrument (n.), cassette tape (n.), CD (n.), VCD (n.), laser disc (n.), DVD (n.)

8·2   1. e (n.)
          2. j (v.)
          3. g (v.)
          4. m (v.)
          5. b (v.)
          6. o (n.)
          7. d (n.)
          8. k (adj.)
          9. n (v.)
          10. a (n.)
          11. f (n.)
          12. h (adj.)
          13. i (v.)
          14. l (n.)
          15. c (v.)

8·3   1. d
          2. f
          3. a
          4. e
          5. b
          6. c

8·4   *Sample sentences:*
1. Faux See-Thru skirts are a recent fashion **craze** in Japan.
2. I'm going to **accompany** my friend on a weekend trip to Vancouver.
3. If you want to get money out of an ATM, you have to **insert** your bank card into the machine first, then enter your PIN.
4. Students who **neglect** to study for an exam will probably fail or get a poor grade.
5. Historians **credit** the Wright Brothers with inventing the airplane.
6. It was a terrible **embarrassment** when I forgot my grandmother's birthday.
7. The West Edmonton Mall is Canada's largest shopping **facility**.
8. You can buy all kinds of **kitschy** souvenirs when you visit Schloss Neuschwanstein.
9. *Awesome* is a word that is really **catching on**; almost everyone uses it.
10. When Susan Boyle sang her **rendition** of "I Dreamed a Dream" on *Britain's Got Talent,* everyone was astounded.
11. Terry Fox's run was a **triumph** of courage and compassion.
12. It is very difficult to get accepted by a **prestigious** university like Harvard or Oxford.
13. Some people believe that chocolate can **bolster** your mood when you're feeling down.
14. The **lyrics** to most of the Beatles' early songs are very easy to understand and sing.
15. All the students in class are **vying** for the attention of the new debate coach.

8·5
1. F
2. T
3. F
4. T
5. T
6. F

8·6
1. empty orchestra
2. a special room that people can rent to sing karaoke
3. in bars, clubs, and karaoke boxes
4. a wide range of pop, country and western, Broadway, and evergreen songs
5. The lyrics appear on a screen with a bouncing ball, so the singer can keep up with the music.
6. It increases oxygen intake and boosts the cardiovascular system; helps us relax and reduce stress; releases endorphins—"feel good" chemicals—into the bloodstream, elevating our mood; can bolster confidence; allows us to express our feelings and to reach out to others.
7. choose a song that suits your voice and vocal range
8. with their diaphragms
9. so they don't strain their vocal cords and sound screechy
10. Smile and sing from your heart.

8·7
1. Daisuke Inoue
2. Roberto del Rosario
3. Kobe
4. Asia
5. 8-track tapes
6. Finland
7. 80,000
8. Finnish
9. ABBA
10. 4.5

8·8
1. No
2. Yes
3. Yes
4. No
5. Yes
6. Yes
7. Yes

8·9 The history of karaoke

    Meaning of *karaoke*: "empty orchestra" in Japanese

    Inventor: Daisuke Inoue, nightclub musician and percussionist, Kobe, Japan; late 1960s

    The first karaoke machine: song track recorded on 8-track tape; box with small amplifier and slot for coins

The popularity of karaoke

    Karaoke venues: bars, nightclubs, restaurants, private clubs, karaoke "boxes," and multistory entertainment complexes

    Karaoke businesses: karaoke entertainment centers, chain stores selling karaoke equipment, special karaoke clubs

    The spread of karaoke: from Japan to Asia in 1990s; later to Europe, North America, and Asia

    Karaoke events and contests: bars host "Karaoke Nights" with theme nights and prizes; Karaoke World Championship established in 2003 in Finland now an international event

The mechanics of karaoke

    Technology: 8-track tapes replaced by cassette tapes; next, CDs, VCDs, laser discs, and DVDs; now available on mobile phones and computers

    Songs: wide choice of pop, country and western, Broadway, and evergreen hits

    Performance: singers can change key, follow lyrics on a screen; some sing on a stage

The benefits of karaoke

    Physiological benefits: good for the heart by increasing oxygen supply to the blood; decreases stress

    Psychological benefits: puts us in a good mood; improves self-confidence; help us express emotions and connect with others

Singing tips

    Choosing a song: choose one that is easy to sing

    Breathing: practice breathing from your diaphragm

    Voice: don't sing too high or strain your vocal cords

    Posture: relax and move with the music

9 The flying doctors of Australia: Reaching "the furthest corner"

9·1 Flying: airborne (adj.), aerial (adj.), aviation (n.), navigate (v.), biplane (n.), flight (n.), airplane (n.), passenger (n.), pilot (n.), cockpit (n.), landing (n.), landing strip (n.), service crew (n.)

Medical services (all n.): ambulance, medical insurance, emergency, clinic, health screening, immunization, mental health care, treatment, medical consultation

Medical equipment (all n.): intensive-care unit, resuscitation device, neonatal incubator, medical oxygen and suction system

9·2
1. d (phr.)
2. g (adj.)
3. l (n./v.)
4. b (n.)
5. n (n.)
6. i (v.)
7. m (n.)
8. e (n./v.)
9. k (v.)
10. a (adj.)
11. h (n./v.)
12. o (v.)
13. f (adj.)
14. c (v.)
15. j (adj.)

9·3
1. treated
2. terrain
3. remote
4. committed
5. conducted
6. urgent
7. witnesses
8. take for granted
9. maintain
10. obstacle
11. vital
12. challenge
13. navigate
14. injuries
15. link

9·4
Paragraph 1: f
Paragraph 2: h
Paragraph 3: c
Paragraph 4: b
Paragraph 5: e
Paragraph 6: a
Paragraph 7: g
Paragraph 8: i
Paragraph 9: d

9·5
1. Presbyterian; Australian Inland Mission; outback
2. medical services
3. Lieutenant Clifford Peel
4. 10
5. business associations; the Presbyterian Church; government agencies; personal supporters
6. Planes could fly a maximum distance of 600 miles at 80 mph; open cockpits exposed pilots to all kinds of weather; pilots had no maps or navigation equipment; there were no fueling stations; pilots had to land on rough terrain with no landing strips; contact between residents and doctors was difficult
7. pedal-operated generator

9·6
1. one doctor; one doctor and one nurse, a second doctor for serious illness or injury
2. 50; 38,852
3. 225; 276,489
4. 26; 74,214
5. 28,968 kilometers; 25,592,455 kilometers
6. 1; 60
7. de Havilland DH.50; King Air, PC-12, Cessna 208B Grand Caravan
8. leased; owned
9. 8 (by 1937); 21 bases
10. 2; 977
11. free; free

9·7
1. He meant that we should ask for the ability to meet the challenges of the work that is important to us rather than asking for jobs that are easy to do.
2. *Mantle* is another word for coat. A "mantle of safety" is a form of security that ensures people's well-being.
3. *Suggested answers:*
   Medical care is available and free to people who do not have insurance.
   Aircraft carry battery-operated emergency equipment for people who are seriously ill or injured.
   The service operates 24 hours a day across Australia.
   A second doctor accompanies the doctor and nurse in cases of serious illness or injury.
   The service offers a wide range of medical services, including immunization and mental health care.

9·8   Our motto: The furthest corner. The finest care.
Our mission: To provide excellence in aeromedical and primary health care across Australia.
Our headquarters: Sydney, New South Wales
Our founder: Reverend John Flynn
Our history
    1928: We flew our first flight as the Australian Inland Mission Aerial Medical Service.
    1930: We changed our name to Aerial Medical Service.
    1942: We became known as the Flying Doctor Service.
    1955: We were officially renamed the Royal Flying Doctor Service.
Our achievements
    We opened sections in every territory in the 1930s.
    We purchased aircraft and hired our own pilots and service crews.
    We continuously update flight and medical equipment.
    We maintain a network of 21 bases, 5 clinics, and 10 offices.
Our staff: Pilots, technicians, doctors, nurses, dentist, aboriginal and Torres Strait health workers,
    and management and administrative staff
Our services
    24-hour emergency and transport services
    General medical care and health care screening
    Immunization and mental health care
    Accident victims treated on-site
    Radio consultations
    Airborne intensive-care units with resuscitation devices, neonatal incubators, and medical oxygen
      and suction systems
    All services free of charge

10   Cirque du Soleil: A dream makes the big time

10·1   Performer: clown, artist, impresario, folk group, musician, fire breather, stilt walker, juggler, dancer,
accordion/harmonica player
Theater: artistic director, producer, festival, storyline, costume designer, smash hit, cast, show, audience,
theatrical troupe

10·2
1. ceremony
2. argument
3. confuse
4. carry on
5. limitation
6. release
7. untruthfulness
8. neglect
9. hopelessness
10. rare
11. dismiss
12. lose
13. underperform
14. fall back
15. solidify

10·3   *Answers will vary.*

10·4
1. creativity
2. isn't
3. can
4. circus
5. artistically successful
6. is
7. stories with characters that deliver a message to the audience
8. are
9. all over the world
10. is

10·5
1. b
2. a
3. a
4. c
5. b
6. c
7. a
8. c
9. b
10. c

10·6
1. c
2. h
3. e
4. i
5. a
6. j
7. b
8. f
9. g
10. d

10·7
1. Yes
2. No
3. No
4. Yes
5. Yes

10·8
The founders: Guy Laliberté and Daniel Gauthier
Company headquarters: Montreal, Quebec, Canada
Its first performance: June 16, 1984, in Gaspé, Quebec
Important contributors and their roles
    Gilles Ste-Croix, first artistic director
    Guy Caron, artistic director
    Franco Dragone, artistic director
    René Dupère, musical scores
    Michel Crête, costume designer
Trademark: Opening with ordinary people transformed into performers
What makes Cirque du Soleil different from other circuses
    Its shows tell stories with messages.
    Each show has a musical score written specifically for it.
    Costumes are designed specifically for each show.
    Shows are like paintings that transcend language barriers.
    The artists come from many countries and cultures.
    The cast includes children.
    Cirque du Soleil focuses on artistic creativity and teamwork.
Awards: Four Primetime Emmys and three Geminis
Number and type of employees: More than 5,000 in 100 different job categories
Number of running shows and venues: 19 shows in 271 cities
Estimated annual revenue: $810 million
Permanent venue: Las Vegas
Circus arts sponsorship: La TOHU, the City of Circus Arts, in Montreal
Community building projects
    The biggest environmental urban waste disposal site in North America
    One Drop Foundation

11 The Findhorn Community: A garden of spirits

11·1 Gardening verbs: dig, plant, grow, thrive, flourish, sow, bloom
Gardening nouns: fertilizer, compost, manure, straw, hay, cold frame, plot, patch
Spirituality: positive thinking, clairvoyant, guidance, meditation, faith, higher power, vibrations,
vision, cosmic energies, spirits

11·2 *Consult a dictionary for definitions.*
1. adj.
2. v.
3. n.
4. adj.
5. adj.
6. v.
7. n.
8. adj.
9. adj.
10. n.
11. v.
12. v.
13. v.
14. v.
15. n.

11·3
1. c
2. c
3. a
4. b
5. c
6. c
7. a
8. c
9. c
10. b
11. c
12. a
13. a
14. b
15. a

11·4
1. they had lost their jobs and it was the only place where they could live in their caravan
2. they had no money and a garden was the only way to feed themselves cheaply
3. the soil was sandy and nothing but gorse, broom, brambles, quitch grass, and spiny trees grew there
4. Eileen had been guided in her meditation to eat less dense and refined food.
5. she was in contact with the Devas and the Landscape Angel, who advised her to radiate love to the plants
6. they could not explain the results in terms of traditional horticulture or organic gardening principles
7. it was a beautiful, harmonious, and spiritual place
8. they cooperated with nature and believed that all plants and beings are part of a greater whole

11·5
1. Findhorn Bay is located in northern Scotland.
2. The Findhorn Bay Caravan Park was located next to a garbage dump.
3. Eileen Caddy and Dorothy Maclean were sensitives.
4. Peter Caddy collected unemployment benefits and welfare to support his family.
5. Peter, Eileen, and Dorothy had no gardening experience.
6. The family changed their diet completely.
7. Eileen meditated in a public washroom when everyone else was asleep.
8. Dorothy made contact with the Devas and Landscape Angel, who gave her gardening instructions.
9. Sir George Trevelyan was astonished at the superior quality of the vegetables and flowers.
10. It took them only five years to establish their garden.

11·6
1. 40 pounds
2. eight feet
3. two feet
4. 65
5. 21
6. more than 40
7. 50 years
8. 300

11·7
1. Negative: The caravan park was run down and next to a garbage dump and had none of the comforts of a real home.
2. Negative: The nicest site in the park was still the complete opposite of the hotel and lifestyle they had been used to.
3. Positive: They received help when they needed it without having to ask or look for it.
4. Negative: Their life looked like it couldn't get any worse, because they had no jobs, no money, and no alternatives.
5. Positive: Their garden was producing far better than anyone had expected.

11·8 *Suggested questions:*
When did you move to Findhorn Bay?
Why did you move there?
What was living in a caravan park like compared to living in a hotel?
What problems did you face in the beginning?
Why did you decide to grow a garden?
What was the secret to growing a garden in poor soil?
How did other people react to the success of your garden?
How has the Findhorn Community developed over the years?
What makes the Findhorn Community special and unique?

12 Aron Ralston: Surviving the worst

12·1 Danger: risk your neck (phr.), treacherous (adj.), in trouble (phr.), predicament (n.), ordeal (n.)
Outdoor activities (all n.): climbing, diving, skiing, jumping, biking, rappelling, exploring
Movement (all v.): dangle, shift, slip, fall, crash, yank, maneuver, budge, jab, squat, hover, crush, smash

12·2
1. confined, confine
2. deprivation, deprive
3. contemplation, contemplative
4. intensification, intense
5. penetration, penetrable OR penetrative
6. aspiration
7. decomposition, decompose
8. encounter
9. ration
10. severance, sever
11. instinct
12. —
13. —
14. —
15. —

12·3
    1. resort to
    2. encountered
    3. deprived
    4. instinctively
    5. decompose
    6. ration
    7. penetrated
    8. excruciating
    9. intensified
   10. aspires
   11. sever
   12. predicament
   13. subsided
   14. confines
   15. contemplating

12·4
    1. T
    2. F (His family and friends didn't know where he had gone, but his colleagues reported him missing after he didn't show up for work.)
    3. T
    4. T
    5. F (Aron took full responsibility for his accident and believed that it was meant to happen.)
    6. F (Aron was able to survive, because he had a vision of himself playing with a three-year-old boy who was to be his son.)

12·5
    9, 4, 10, 2, 8, 13, 6, 12, 1, 5, 7, 3, 11

12·6
    1. c
    2. b
    3. c
    4. b
    5. a
    6. c
    7. b
    8. b
    9. c
   10. a

12·7
    1. would be
    2. had a feeling
    3. The rock
    4. took responsibility
    5. couldn't be saved
    6. *Suggested answer:* Our higher goal in life is to pursue what makes us truly happy, to find what we deeply care about, and to live our lives as an example for other people.

12·8   *Answers will vary.*

13 Harry Potter: More than magic

13·1 Popularity: beloved, fans, devotees, fanatics, mania, success, wildfire, acclaim, onslaught, exuberance

Books: pages, chapters, title, author, writer, story, characters, translation, copy, edition

Publishing: manuscript, bestseller, literary agent/agency, publisher, release, reviews, signing, schedule, best-seller list, book awards/prizes

13·2
1. v., criticism
2. v., dislike
3. v., finish
4. v., not see
5. v., cancel
6. v., run behind
7. v., accept
8. v., do without
9. n., everyday event
10. n., small amount
11. v., neglect
12. v., find immediately
13. v., destroy
14. adj., known
15. n., normal person

13·3
1. spawned
2. outpace
3. cherished
4. phenomenon
5. wizard
6. launched
7. scouted around
8. rejects
9. acclaim
10. debuted
11. promote
12. rely on
13. envisioned
14. unanticipated
15. proliferation

13·4
Paragraph 1: c
Paragraph 2: l
Paragraph 3: e
Paragraph 4: g
Paragraph 5: a
Paragraph 6: i
Paragraph 7: d
Paragraph 8: h
Paragraph 9: f
Paragraph 10: b
Paragraph 11: j
Paragraph 12: k

13·5   1. F (She thought up the story of Harry Potter while she was on a commuter train in England.)
        2. F (Rowling had been writing for herself since childhood.)
        3. T
        4. T
        5. F (It was Rowling's publisher's idea to change her name to J. K. Rowling.)
        6. F (Sales of *Harry Potter and the Philosopher's Stone* hit 70,000 in the first year.)
        7. T
        8. F (Her books sold just as well in the US as they did in the UK.)
        9. T
       10. T
       11. F (*Harry Potter* books were popular with adults.)
       12. T
       13. F (They have been popular all over the world in English and in translation.)
       14. F (Her first signing tour in the US was not a success—it was a nonevent.)
       15. T

13·6   1. g
        2. a
        3. d
        4. b
        5. a
        6. c
        7. e
        8. f
        9. g
       10. a

13·7   1. b
        2. b
        3. b
        4. a
        5. b
        6. a
        7. b
        8. a

13·8   *Answers will vary.*

14   The Paralympics: Believe in yourself

14·1   Disabilities: paraplegic, spinal cord injury, amputee/amputation, congenital defect/deformity, cerebral palsy, multiple sclerosis, muscular dystrophy, spina bifida, dwarfism, polio, blindness, myleodysplasia
        Sports events: archery, track, throwing, marathon, pentathlon, goalball, football/soccer, hockey, skiing, biathlon, dance, fencing, tennis, table tennis, volleyball, basketball, rugby, curling

14·2   1. d (v.)
        2. i (v.)
        3. n (v.)
        4. b (v)
        5. g (n.)
        6. k (v.)
        7. e (adj.)
        8. l (n.)
        9. h (v.)
       10. a (n.)
       11. m (v.)
       12. f (v.)
       13. o (v.)
       14. c (v.)
       15. j (n.)

14·3
1. expand, expansion
2. accommodation, accommodate
3. advocacy, advocates
4. classified, classification
5. competed, competition
6. domination, dominated
7. elite, elitist
8. evaluation, evaluate
9. enrichment, enrich
10. impairs, impairment
11. participate, participation
12. modifications, modify
13. requires, requirement
14. rehabilitation, rehabilitate
15. therapy, therapeutic

14·4
1. c
2. b
3. b
4. a
5. a
6. c
7. a
8. c

14·5
1. The first official competition for athletes with disabilities was held in 1948 in London, England.
2. Dr. Ludwig Guttmann, the "father of sport for people with disabilities," organized the International Stoke Mandeville Games in England.
3. The first officially recognized Paralympic Games were held in 1960 in Rome, Italy.
4. The first Paralympic Winter Games took place in Sweden in 1976.
5. The Paralympics are overseen by the International Paralympic Committee in Düsseldorf, Germany.
6. Paralympic athletes are classified according to physical, visual, and intellectual disabilities, and these are broken down into six categories: amputees, those with spinal cord injuries, those with cerebral palsy, those with visual impairment, those with intellectual impairment, and Les Autres.
7. Athletes are evaluated by classifiers with specialized medical and technical knowledge.
8. There are 20 sports in the summer games and 5 in the winter games.
9. In the biathlon event, the rifle is specially modified for visually impaired participants.
10. Football-7-a-side was designed for athletes with cerebral palsy or neurological impairments, and goalball for athletes with visual impairments.

14·6
1. archery
2. 1992; Albertville, France; 1998; Seoul, South Korea
3. 22, Nordic skiing
4. Trischa Zorn
5. Sweden; cerebral palsy, multiple sclerosis, spinal injury, double-leg amputation, or any impairment confining their mobility
6. six, bells
7. sit-ski
8. track and field
9. Beijing, 4,011, 146
10. 2000 Summer; Sydney, Australia

14·7
1. c
2. a
3. a
4. b
5. c

14·8   History of the Paralympics

Founder: Dr. Ludwig Guttmann

His reason: to use sports therapy to increase physical strength and self-worth in his patients and to enrich their quality of life

First competition for adults with disabilities: the International Wheelchair Games held in London, England, on July 29, 1948

1952: Stoke Mandeville Games included Dutch servicemen

1960: International Stoke Mandeville Games officially recognized as the Paralympic Games in Rome with 400 participating athletes from 24 countries

1976: first Paralympic Winter Games held in Örnsköldsvik, Sweden

2008: 4,011 athletes from 146 countries took part in 20 sports and 472 events in the Summer Paralympic Games in Beijing

Disabilities and impairments: amputees, spinal cord injuries, cerebral palsy, les autres, visual impairment, intellectual impairment

Paralympic events: athletics, goalball, football-7-a-side, ice sledge hockey, skiing, biathlon, wheelchair events

Paralympic heroes: Trischa Zorn, Ragnhild Myklebust, Li Duan, Louise Sauvage

Positive impact: companies more likely to hire disabled people, more wheelchair access to public buildings and places, disabled people receive equal status

15   Superman: Everyone's superhero

15·1   Nouns: savior, good guy, alter ego, strongmen
Adjectives: heroic, charismatic, invulnerable, hunky, glamorous, swashbuckling

15·2   *Consult a dictionary for definitions.*
1. accomplished, accomplish
2. claim
3. compensatory, compensate
4. distressed OR distressful, distress
5. exposed, expose
6. exploited OR exploitable, exploit
7. accumulation, accumulative
8. approach, approachable
9. diminution, diminish
10. reinstatement
11. spin-off
12. suspect OR suspicion, suspicious
13. conscientious
14. suit
15. torment

15·3   *Suggested answers:*
1. The computer is one of mankind's greatest scientific accomplishments.
2. You can accumulate _____ points when you play your favorite video or computer game.
3. The barometric pressure falls when bad weather is approaching.
4. You can submit claims for items that are stolen or lost in transit.
5. When people are injured in an accident, they can receive compensation in the form of money.
6. When my conscience bothers me, I feel bad or guilty.
7. The population of some wild animals is diminishing because of global warming.
8. SOS, or May Day, is the international distress signal.
9. Exposure to chemicals can cause serious health problems.
10. They like to read about the exploits of explorers and adventurers, because the stories are interesting and exciting.
11. If someone is fired from his job without a good reason, the person should be reinstated.
12. Up to 400 different products were spun off from the *Harry Potter* series.
13. If one person wants to sue another person, he needs the help of a lawyer.
14. If my cell phone were stolen, I would suspect one of my classmates.
15. Bullies torment other students, because it makes them feel powerful.

15·4
1. changed
2. has become
3. is
4. never gave up
5. haven't stayed
6. has represented
7. is

15·5
1. Jerry Siegel and Joe Shuster
2. Superman's alter ego and reporter for the *Daily Planet*
3. The Man of Steel
4. Detective Comics, Inc. in 1938
5. Because he aided ordinary people in distress and fought against social evils of the time, such as unjust imprisonment, domestic abuse, corruption, labor problems, and disarmament
6. Batman and Robin, the Flash, the Green Lantern, Superboy, and Supergirl
7. *Superman, Action Comics, The World's Finest Comics,* and *All Star Comics*
8. The Golden Age, the Silver Age, the Bronze Age, and the Steel Age
9. In newspapers, on radio and television, and in movies
10. From the radio show *The Adventures of Superman*

15·6
1. 1993
2. 2006
3. 1940
4. 1953
5. 1998
6. 1978
7. 1993
8. 1938
9. 1962
10. 1999

15·7
1. No
2. Yes
3. No
4. No
5. No

15·8
Birth name: Kal-El
Place of birth: Planet Krypton
Birth father: Jor-El
Human name: Clark Kent
Adoptive parents: Jonathan and Martha Kent
Hometown: Smallville, Kansas
Wife's name: Lois Lane
Job: Newspaper reporter for the *Daily Planet*
Personality of Clark Kent: Myopic, socially awkward, meek, intelligent, hard-working, decent
Superpowers: Can fly; has X-ray, telescopic, and microscopic vision; is invulnerable to atomic fallout; is faster than a speeding bullet; is more powerful than a locomotive; can leap tall buildings in a single bound
Weakness: Is vulnerable to kryptonite
Costume: A bright blue suit with a red cape and a diamond-shaped *S* emblazoned on his chest
Colleagues: Jimmy Olsen and Lois Lane
Friends: Batman and Robin, Supergirl
Enemies: The Ultra-Humanite, the Archer, the Puzzler, the Prankster, the Toyman, Mr. Mxyztplk, J. Wilbur Wolfingham, Bizarro, Brainiac, Lex Luthor
Mission: To fight for truth, justice, and the American way of life
Feats and accomplishments: Aids ordinary people in distress; fights against crime syndicates, evil megalomaniacs, and alien forces with superpowers of their own